J.L. BARKAS, Ph.D.

4.77

CREATIVE
TIME
MANAGEMENT

Become More Productive
and Still Have Time for Fun

training & development

A SPECTRUM BOOK

Prentice-Hall, Inc., Englewood Cliffs, N.J. 07632

Library of Congress Cataloging in Publication Data

BARKAS, J. L.
    Creative time management.

    A Spectrum Book.
    Bibliography: p.
    Includes index.
    1. Time management. I. Title.
HD38.B243 1984   646.7   84-9851
ISBN   0-13-191222-4
ISBN   0-13-191214-3 (pbk.)

This book is available at a special discount when ordered in bulk quantities. Contact Prentice-Hall, Inc., General Publishing Division, Special Sales, Englewood Cliffs, N. J. 07632.

A SPECTRUM BOOK

Manufacturing buyer: Edward J. Ellis
Cover design © 1984 by Jeannette Jacobs

ISBN 0-13-191214-3 {PBK.}

ISBN 0-13-191222-4

10 9 8 7 6 5 4 3 2

Printed in the United States of America

For my friend Nona

The names and identifying details of the examples used in this book have been changed to protect the anonymity of those interviewed. Any resemblance to any person, living or dead, is coincidental. This book provides the author's opinions on the subjects it covers. It is sold with the understanding that neither the publisher nor the author is engaged in providing medical, legal, counseling, or other professional service. If medical, legal, or other expert help is necessary, the services of a competent professional should be sought.

PRENTICEHALL INTERNATIONAL, INC., *London*
PRENTICE-HALL OF AUSTRALIA PTY. LIMITED, *Sydney*
PRENTICE-HALL OF CANADA INC., *Toronto*
PRENTICE-HALL OF INDIA PRIVATE LIMITED, *New Delhi*
PRENTICE-HALL OF JAPAN, INC., *Tokyo*
PRENTICE-HALL OF SOUTHEAST ASIA PTE. LTD., *Singapore*
WHITEHALL BOOKS LIMITED, *Wellington, New Zealand*
EDITORA PRENTICE-HALL DO BRASIL LTDA., *Rio de Janeiro*

Contents

Preface   v

1

Personal and Work Time Management:
An Introduction   1

2

Obstacles to Effective Time Management   19

3

Becoming Organized and More Effective   47

4

Improving Your Time at Work   67

5

Saving Time on Household Chores   89

6

Improving Your Personal Time Management   103

7

How Time Management Works   121

Appendices   137

    Appendix I: The ABC Approach   138

    Appendix II: Daily Activity Schedule   139

    Appendix III: An Ideal Day   140

    Appendix IV: Time Management Self-Evaluation   141

    Appendix V: Planning Chart   143

    Appendix VI: Student Checklist   144

    Appendix VII: Time Management for Teachers   145

    Appendix VIII: Creating Your Own
    Time Management Solutions   146

Index   147

Preface

In researching this book I discovered a common time management problem shared by those who are always busy but never able to accomplish as much as they want: They are reactive, rather than active, persons. They react to external demands on them, whether for a report due on Friday or a party they are invited to on Saturday, rather than acting according to long-term goals they have set for themselves within which most short-term decisions are made. Furthermore, the necessity to prioritize what is important is clearest when they get attacks of the "if onlys" ("I wouldn't have been late if only I hadn't answered the phone on my way out," "If only I hadn't gone to the movies when I wanted to finish writing that report") as well as during those moments of pride when the rewards are clearest (having work done on time, graduating from school).

Through my interviews I discovered that most men and women share the same goal: a full life, not a life that is weighted too heavily toward either work or leisure. The man who never exercises or does anything for himself (until he has a heart attack) because he is attending to his job and family is someone in need of creative time management as much as the woman who is juggling all her balls so vigorously—spouse, job, children—that she lacks a moment to put up her feet and just relax.

Initially there may be frustrations when you take charge of your life and time. However, you will quickly see benefits as well, not to mention the permanent and greater long-term gains. This is not the same thing as becoming so narcissistic that everything and everyone is measured by "What does this time demand mean to *me?*" Sometimes, for example, it may be in your best interest to put others before yourself; sometimes not. Example: You are working on an important assignment. The phone rings. Your friend is upset and wants to talk for ten minutes. You say you don't have the time. Your friend is disappointed. You have that ten minutes for your work, but in the long run, was working on your report the best use of those ten minutes?

The goal of *Creative Time Management* is to help you make those crucial judgments about how you spend your time. By maximizing the gains from ways you spend your time in work, school, or leisure situations (at meetings, while commuting, on the telephone, when socializing), as well as understanding the most common time wasters (procrastination, complaining, fear of success or of failure, doing too many things at once) you will see distinct improvements in what you are accomplishing, and how you feel. As each day is spent more efficiently and creatively, you will achieve more in the short-run, as well as attaining more of your long-range work and personal goals. That will all add up to a more fulfilling life.

How one manages one's time will depend on where one is in one's life cycle, which, today, has a wider variation than even, say, twenty years ago. A thirty-two-year old woman gives up her job in Manhattan as a fiction editor at a leading women's magazine to relocate to Colorado and begin medical school. A sixty-year old man gives up smoking and devotes more time to exercise and self-improvement than at any time since his days on the track team in high school. A forty-year-old woman, faced with her teenager's imminent departure from home, rethinks where she and her husband want to live and the kind of full-time work she wants to do till her retirement.

Prioritizing can be stressful when you temporarily disappoint those who are counting on you because you put something or someone else first. Often it is only in hindsight, thrilled that a plan "worked," that others can see its justification. (Another plan might have worked as well. There is, of course, no *one* way of managing one's time. There are concrete indicators, however, as to whether your plans have worked, or are working.)

There are practical tips about managing your time that will give you more minutes or even months of additional time than you may currently have available to you. The phone can be a terrific time saver; for most of us, it wastes hours of time and interrupts projects and in-person conversations. Doing the paper shuffle can consume lots of valuable time; managing your files well could be a time saver. Getting organized refers to such specific techniques as creating a "things to do" list; it also involves learning more basic organizing principles that will help you to organize your life, not just your books and files.

Creative Time Management will show you how you can effectively manage your time. It will help you pinpoint how you currently manage your time, how you would like to manage it, what's stopping you, and ways to achieve your "ideal" for work, school, or leisure periods.

ACKNOWLEDGMENTS

I had been researching and writing newspaper articles related to time management when Lynne Lumsden of Prentice-Hall, Inc. and Allan Lang and Maureen Rolla of International Book Marketing, Ltd. approached me in 1980 about writing a book on the subject. From the very beginning of this project I conceived of time management as life management; the original research I conducted therefore looked at concepts about time as well as managing time at work, school, home, and in leisure settings. Lynne Lumsden's editorial assistant, Denise Andriello-Higgins, patiently saw this manuscript through to completion and an anonymous reviewer for Prentice-Hall contributed valuable comments that helped me to improve the final book.

Richard B. Hoffman assisted by editing and proofreading an early draft of this manuscript. Robyn Goldstein initially suggested adding *Creative* to the title of this book. Patricia Mangiapane, Dave and Lil Schaeffer, Wendy Silverman, Martin Edelston, Steven H. Gruenberg, Martin Greenberg, James O'Shea Wade, Marilyn Machlowitz, and Jean Barish kindly read and commented on chapters or entire drafts of this manuscript.

Those who completed my questionnaire and granted telephone or in-person interviews, although anonymous in this text, were indispensable to the final book. I also want to thank the numerous experts who granted me interviews or corresponded with me, some who are quoted by name in the text, for their time and interest. Those authors and their publishers are also thanked whose excerpted material appears in this book. Where appropriate, attribution was made in the text (and a full citation appears in the bibliography at the end of the chapter). I am, however, responsible—and must take the credit or blame—for everything else in this book.

Finally, I want to thank those friends, family members, and colleagues who stood by me patiently as I learned how to manage my time more effectively so I could accomplish more, yet have more time to be with the people that I care about. Special thanks to: my parents, Dr. William and Gladys Barkas, Eileen B. Hoffman, Karen Lobovits, Mary Tierney, Nona Aguilar, Gail Schiller Tuchman, Ellis B. Levine, Matt Silverman, Bernie Koster, Ginny Mugavero, C. H. Rolph, Ina Caro, Joyce Guy Patton, Joan Freyberg, Ed Speedling, Maxine Wallach, Daniele Levine, Richard Snider, Joyce Bronstein, Diana Levine, Phyllis Henkel, Carol Ann Finkelstein, and Pramila Poddar.

1
Personal and Work Time Management: An Introduction

Lost time is never found again.

BENJAMIN FRANKLIN
(*Poor Richard's Almanac*)

Managing your time well means managing your life well. A great deal can be accomplished in twenty-four hours a day, or not much at all. It's up to you to make good use of those hours. We are not all endowed with brains, good looks, or lots of money, but we each get the same twenty-four hours in a day—no more, no less. You might envy one of your friends, who somehow finds the time to give lavish dinner parties, and wonder how she also avoids being in hot water at the office for lateness. You might admire Fred for his rapid rise at the brokerage firm, and be impressed that he also finds time to spend with his family. You might wish you too could put in a productive day at work and rush off to a party or movie—but when you've tried "doing it all," your professional or personal performance suffered.

People who exemplify creative time management do exist; they are not Supermen or Superwomen. What they do, and what you can do too, is clarify goals so that as many priorities as possible can be accomplished.

Why is better time management so important? Poor time management causes missed deadlines, unfinished projects, disappointed employers, cancelled appointments, burnt pot roast, miffed friends, and postponed vacations. Mismanagement of time can also lead to low self-esteem, depression, unfulfilled career aspirations, children growing up strangers to their parents (and vice versa), potential friendships that never progress past acquaintanceships, such self-destructive habits as overeating, smoking, and inactivity, and even unsatisfactory sex lives ("I'm too tired tonight, dear," "I've got too much on my mind", or most pertinent of all, "Not enough time!").

Slogans—"Make every day count," "Live each day as if it were your last," "Life is a process, not an event"—provide overall philosophies; they do not tell you how to apply those philosophies to daily life. An accurate definition of your current activities and your desired outcomes is fundamental to achieving those outcomes.

A simple and effective way to look at how you manage your time is the "A B C" approach:

(A)   KNOWING WHAT YOU'VE GOT.
(B)   KNOWING WHAT YOU WANT.
(C)   USING (A) AND (B) SO YOU GET WHAT YOU WANT.

Knowing what you've got means having a clear view of your present work and personal situations. Knowing what you want means having specific daily and long-term goals. Getting what you want requires that you apply to your thoughts and actions the questions that journalists ask when writing a story, namely: WHO, WHAT, WHEN, WHERE, and HOW. Fulfilling your goals is also aided by asking a sixth question, one that social scientists apply to their research, namely: WHY. By understanding how to apply this six-word analysis to your activities, you will improve the way you manage your time.

Fortunately, effective time management is a skill that can be learned. Unlike genius in music or precocity in mathematics, expertise in time management uses skills that can be acquired and improved. Thus, for most of us, developing effective time management techniques means unlearning poor habits (usually acquired haphazardly) and replacing them with more purposeful, better-systematized patterns. The payoff is not only greater satisfaction in one's work, school, and personal activities but better performance and, ultimately, greater achievement of goals in life as well. Ironically it is those who effectively manage their time who appear more relaxed and self-satisfied; it is those who are constantly underestimating how long something will take, or who are poor planners, who seem frenzied, driven, and in terror of "the clock."

If you suddenly could do whatever your heart desired, what would you do—or, to put it another way, how would you manage your time? For all of us, how we handle our non-obligatory hours is at least as important as how we deal with the demands of work or school.

Consider the concept of time, and some time-related expressions that are familiar to us all:

"I never have enough time."
"What time does the party begin?"
"He's never on time."
"I always have a good time with you."

"He wrote his thesis in record time."
"What time should I call you back?"

Time is a cultural concept. Westerners, for example, think in terms of twenty-four hours in a day, and seven days in a week. However, those divisions are arbitrary. There is no such thing as "a week"; we have invented that concept. Time is a concept that varies greatly from culture to culture, within each culture, and even between individuals. The workday, for example, will differ for an office worker in Manhattan, for whom it may start at nine, and for one in Lima, Peru, for whom it may begin before eight. Students view time away from classrooms during the summer months far differently than typical workers who are still in their offices.

In *The Dance of Life: The Other Dimension of Time,* Edward T. Hall contrasts the way AE people ("people of American-European heritage") think about time with time concepts in other cultures, like the Hopi Indians whose reservations he first visited in 1931. In summarizing the differences between the Hopi, who live "in the eternal present," and AE peoples, Hall writes: ". . . One feels that [for the Hopi] time is not a harsh taskmaster nor is it equated with money and progress as it is with AE peoples. . . . Whites tend to think that because nothing overt is happening, nothing is going on. With many cultures there are long periods during which people are making up their minds or waiting for a consensus to be achieved. We would do well to pay more attention to these things."

Sociologist Eviatar Zerubavel heeds the same warning. In *Hidden Rhythms: Schedules and Calendars in Social Life,* Zerubavel cautions: ". . . We are increasingly detaching ourselves from 'organic and functional periodicity,' which is dictated by nature, and replacing it by 'mechanical periodicity,' which is dictated by the schedule, the calendar, and the clock." Few, for example, take a vacation because they "need to"; most people have to schedule time off from work weeks or months ahead. When that scheduled time arrives, however, they may wish they could somehow go later on (or regret failing to have taken time off sooner).

Won't it all work out somehow if you can just "muddle through"? Stop and think for a minute. As the demands on your time have changed in your life, have you adjusted your time budget to reflect those changes? Do you even have a time budget? Perhaps you have just had a child, you just got married, you have a vacation coming up in two weeks, or you've started night school. Did you, to accommodate those changes, shift your activities? Maybe it was not so recently that a change occurred—you got promoted, you switched jobs, your friend moved out-of-town—but you are still managing your time in the same old way. Or maybe you're just sick and tired of always being "busy" but never really accomplishing anything that means that much to you. It may just be that you don't want to have to apologize again for having to cancel a meeting with a friend, or for keeping a valued customer waiting.

Those who handle their time well do it creatively; they show certain characteristics that separate them from those who are usually in a state of unprepared frenzy. This book will help you to develop those time-effective habits—like short- and long-term planning, setting and keeping realistic schedules, taking efficiency breaks, and viewing tasks to be done as opportunities, not dreaded obligations. If you feel your time management needs improvement, you can change—if you really want to. You may need to alter the way you view your time, your work, your personal commitments, and your hobbies, or you may only need to buy a daily calendar in which to record your current and future appointments. The benefits of "doing it right" are quickly observed—by you and by others—and that reinforcement encourages you to make those changes stick, and to go further. You will wonder at how you ever tolerated so much wasted time before: time you could have spent doing something else—reading, fishing, dancing, day-dreaming—whatever your pleasure.

Effective time management may mean different things during work and during personal time. In doing housework or schoolwork, you may want to do more in less time—so you can spend more time pursuing your own interests. By contrast, nine-to-five realities may mean that even if you finish your day's work in three hours, you can't leave the office and go fishing. Even so, you'll get a lot more work done—without staying late!

A consistent theme of this book will be that there is no one right way to manage your time. Accomplishment is not the sole measure of effective time management; executives may achieve their professional goals at great cost to health, personal activities, and relationships. With creative time management, the same goals can be met, but with added time for leisure activities, as well as improved (and more satisfying) personal relationships. Workaholism is often a symptom of poor time management: an inability to begin, pursue, and complete a project leads the workaholic to focus solely on the project. The squeaky wheel gets all the grease and the other wheels get none; the job becomes all. As one reluctant workaholic somewhat breathlessly put it, "I keep working around the clock because I hope somehow I'll get everything done so someday I won't have to work so hard." Pacing yourself, and gaining control of your time, lets you accomplish what you value at work, in school, or at home, and gives you more time for friends, family, and leisure activities. It also helps avert burn-out—total loss of initiative or of the ability to continue work toward accomplishing the task at hand. Poor time management can cause the burn-out syndrome; even if some key goals are achieved, it is only at enormous personal and professional cost.

Warren, 32, a health care professional, practices effective time management at his job; he takes Wednesdays, Saturdays, and Sundays off each week. "Taking Wednesdays off gives me the ability, energy, and incentive to do my best when I *am* at work," he explains. "It makes a difference." Sometimes his friends suggest that he would earn more money by working more days; he feels it might be a short-lived gain, since the quality of his work might suffer, along with his job satisfaction.

Being effective does not always mean working longer, or harder. It may even mean working fewer hours; it may mean changing where and when you work, or it may mean trying to do something in a different way.

Do more by working *smarter.*

Consider a married woman of twenty-nine who had her first child last year. A child care worker looks after the infant while she and her husband are at their offices. Before the baby was born, she was in her office by eight, and did not leave till six-thirty or seven each evening. Now, because of the baby, she does not arrive till nine, and always leaves by five. "I'm amazed that I don't find that my productivity has suffered," she told me. "A lot of that early and late stuff was for show. The only difference now is that I return more phone calls the next day, rather than right away, but I've found the calls can wait until the next day." Although some managers may disagree about the wisdom of letting calls wait, she feels she has adjusted her time to manage her work- and home-related responsibilities more effectively, even though she now has more demands on her time.

SETTING GOALS

If you don't know where you'd like to go, how can you know how to get there, why you're trying to get there, or even when you've gotten there? Obviously, you can't. Goals are necessary, at work, school, or play. Without them you flounder, and react erratically to opportunities and problems, with little perspective on the effects they will have on your personal and professional life. Do you have a grand scheme? At certain times in life it's easier to realize that you need a master plan—for example, when you're in high school and practically everyone is making major life decisions—whether to go to college, to pursue a particular career, to get married or to postpone that commitment till after college. Once a course is decided upon, law school or nursing, for example, and once a career is started, it's easy to get caught up in the day-to-day pressures of survival: earning a living, dating or marrying, and raising a family. The time for a "grand scheme" may seem to be behind you.

It's not! No matter what age you are, you can develop daily, weekly, yearly, or longer-range goals to guide you. That does not mean becoming such a future-oriented person that you fail to enjoy the present. What it does mean is that by setting goals you can better manage your life today.

Setting goals facilitates effective time management. Knowing what you want to do makes it easier to achieve those goals. Ask yourself the question that has made time expert Alan Lakein, author of *How To Get Control Of Your Time and Your Life*, a success: *"what is the best use of my time right now?"* If you have goals, you can examine what you are now doing and its relationship to achieving those goals. This system will work whether you use it for daily, weekly, or yearly decisions. Everything you decide to do—or to avoid—is measured against your goals. You no longer have to ruminate about each and every intrusion, opportunity, or question. You have a useful formula on which to base your "yes" and "no" decisions.

Suppose you have a report to write—it's due in a week—but you just got a call from a friend asking you to visit him in California. Should you stop writing the report and fly out to the West Coast? Should you catch the next plane, packing some working papers and what you have written so far? Should you rush to finish the job, and then fly away? Should you say no to the trip? You can't really decide till you assess how a current goal—writing the report—and how the trip fits into your present and long-term goals.

What are your long-term goals? Take a few moments to think about them. What do you hope to be doing in five years? Ten years? Twenty years? If that's too far ahead for you to plan, how about one year from today? Six months? Next month? Next week? Take time to take stock of yourself—from where you live, earn your living, and spend your spare time, to your friendships and love relationships. Set goals; it will help you in the daily management of your time. Use the space below to write down two important long-term goals—one in your career and one in your personal life.

Career Goal:

_____

Personal Goal:

_____

How Do You *Now* Manage Your Time?

Personal Time Management Inventories
Are you aware of the precise way you now use your time? For instance, you might be at work from nine to five, leaving your home by seven and

returning by six-thirty in the evening, but how many hours during the day do you spend on the phone? reading the newspaper? talking to co-workers? reading mail? answering mail? getting to appointments? making new contacts?

If you want to change your use of time, you have to go about it the way you would if you wanted to lose or gain weight: you need to know what your eating (time) habits really are. Your goal is not a "crash course" in more effective time management because, as in dieting, the results will be short-lived. Your goal is permanent change. Just as keeping a food diary helps you see where and when the calories attack, keeping a time diary will enable you to confront—in black and white—how you spend (or waste) your time.

Start by finding out how you think you spend your time by creating a "day before" diary. To the best of your ability, write down how you think you spent yesterday, whether it was a work day or a leisure day. Be as specific as possible, noting when you woke up, got to your work place (or to class), got the children off to school, made trips to the duplicating machine, and called friends or colleagues. Use a blank sheet of paper to create your own inventory, or try the sample that follows in this chapter.

Today's Inventory.   Now begin an inventory, or time log, for today. Carry it through until this time tomorrow. Below is a sample inventory to use as a model.

Daily Time Log

Date: _____

TIME	*ACTIVITY*
_____	_____
_____	_____
_____	_____
_____	_____
_____	_____
_____	_____
_____	_____
_____	_____
_____	_____
_____	_____

Write down every activity that you engage in, from studying and work-related activities to watching TV, talking on the phone, writing letters, reading, preparing and eating meals, talking with your family and friends, daydreaming, making love, and sleeping. You may wish to continue this personal time inventory for the remainder of the week, but even one day's record will provide you with a great deal of specific information.

After you finish your daily log, go back and circle those activities that you *had* to do (e.g., dictating letters, cleaning your home, sleeping, eating, studying, making business calls). Then, with a different colored pencil or pen, circle those activities that you *wanted* to do (e.g., reading a mystery, going to the movies, engaging in sports, playing with children, making love).

Add up the total number of hours spent in groups of activities and place those numbers in the spaces provided below:

_____ Sleeping and eating

_____ Personal maintenance (e.g., washing hair, getting dressed, shaving)

_____ Traveling to and from work or school

_____ Work/school activities

_____ Leisure activities

_____ Watching TV

Now look over your inventory *and* your daily totals. How much time during the day and evening do you spend on necessary activities, such as sleeping, commuting, and getting dressed, and how much time is left over for work and personal commitments? How many hours were spent productively working? How many hours in enjoyable leisure activities? How many hours on the phone?

Reflect on the day you chronicled. What were your main goals that day? Write them down. Are there distinct differences between what you had hoped to accomplish and what you actually did achieve?

Understanding how you now manage your time is the first step toward changing those habits that foster poor time management.

Look back over the goals that you wrote down. How long before the day that you inventoried were you thinking about those goals? *Remember that the reason you want to achieve specific goals each day*—e.g., put material together for a report, prepare a low-calorie dinner—*relates to other, longer-term goals*—e.g., approval from boss, trying to lose fifteen pounds.

"But I didn't really have specific goals," you may say. "Getting to work and doing my job" is a goal, of sorts, but not the kind of goal that will help you more effectively manage your time. What you need to learn to do—or, if you do it already, to do in an even better way—is to plan.

Reconsider your time management concerns. Do have a better idea of (A)—KNOW WHAT YOU'VE GOT? Well, you know that you've got twenty-four hours each day to work with. You may even now know how many hours a day you spend sleeping, eating, reading the newspaper, getting to and from work, in meetings, watching TV, etc. To more effectively manage your time you also want to learn more specific personality traits that you've got—an inability to take criticism, a fear of failure, being too perfectionistic, etc. Those traits, and many more, will be discussed, with suggestions for how to change them, in the next chapter. For now, however, take the time to consider (B)—KNOW WHAT YOU WANT. Whether it's making the most of today or tomorrow, this year, or the rest of your life, planning helps, as does knowing how to best utilize your energy and reduce fatigue and stress.

How Do You *Want* To Manage Your Time?

Planning and Scheduling

One consequence for those rushed Americans who live by the clock is poor planning. Everyday concerns—what some time management experts, such as Robert D. Rutherford, refer to as LOPOs (low-payoff activities)—are given priority at the expense of the more important, long-term goals or HIPOs (high-payoff activities). *A way to counteract that tendency is by creating long-term plans and, within those plans, short-term priorities.*

Why is time planning infrequently or inconsistently done? Most of us fail to plan because we are action-oriented. Planning will, however, affect the very actions that you will take, and effective time managers agree that planning leads to more thoughtful actions. As experts Alex Mackenzie and Kay Cronkite Waldo note in *About Time!*: "When problems arise, you want to be involved in solving them . . . So planning is neglected, which means that even more problems will arise, necessitating even more firefighting and crisis management."

How often have you wanted to go away for a weekend, but because you waited too long found that you could not get reservations? You vow that next time you'll plan better, and reap the benefits. The most common example of poor planning is lateness—failing to get to an appointment on time, handing a report in a month or two overdue, arriving after the movie began. Effective planning does not mean rigidity or inflexibility; it means maximizing results by having control of your time (and life).

By now you have completed one or more daily inventories (time logs) that have revealed how you currently spend your time. Let's move on toward attaining your goal of more effective time management. You should have established, or be in the process of formulating, long-term plans—a one-year, five-year, or even ten-year plan. With those long-term goals in mind, you can now consider shorter goals, from within six months to next month to tomorrow.

Most of us are aware of how workday and weekend (or time off) goals and activities differ. There are, however, more finite differences among workdays than you may realize. (Or you may want to create your own time management "rules" for Mondays versus Tuesdays or Fridays, recognizing the demands and rhythms for each day.) Rules that fit your goals, personality, and energy highs and lows will result in more productive use of your time. Jim, 32, an editor in a publishing house, follows this rule: "I make it a policy to call my authors and my mother back the same day." That "rule" reaffirms the trust of those who work with him. (By contrast, you may decide your job demands a different kind of rule, such as, "I will not receive, or make, any personal phone calls from the office.") Rules may be imposed by your boss: "This is a nine to five job, not nine to four-thirty." You may have, or want to begin, formalizing your own rules: "I will write a two-hundred-word summary of my accomplishments at work last week." Rethink your preconceived notions of planning and consider planning an ally, not a rigid taskmaster.

Using Your Energy Highs and Lows. One way to improve the way that you plan and schedule a day is to become aware of your personal energy highs and lows. No two persons have the same biological rhythms—your neighbor may thrive on five hours of sleep a night but you feel like a zombie unless you get eight. After years of experimentation with various ways of structuring my time, I have discovered that I can do quite well on only six hours of sleep; I must also consider my energy levels, which enable me to work in long and hard spurts, with few or no interruptions, rather than breaking, even for the phone. When are *your* energy highs?

Author Flora Davis shares the conclusions that she reached in *Living Alive!,* as well as how she uses her own energy highs and lows:

> Every system in the body, whether you're talking about the pulse, or the temperature, or the functioning of the endocrine glands, goes through a twenty-four hour cycle. There's a time when it peaks, and these are predictable periods. When the body temperature is low, you are at your lowest in terms of efficiency and alertness. Most people probably don't have to take their temperature to know when that time is for them. Most people know if they're an afternoon or a morning person. But what a lot of people don't know is that it's a physical phenomenon, and there are real reasons for it. For example, I know that it takes me till ten o'clock in the morning to get going, and it has for as many years as I can remember. So I read the newspaper at that time, which doesn't take as much concentration or energy as other tasks.

A primary consideration in planning and scheduling your day is, therefore, whether you are a morning, afternoon, or evening type of person (or some combination of the three). Try to plan your time within your own energy cycles. Another concern is how much sleep *you* need. You may need ten hours, or only four; there is no absolute rule about needing eight hours a day.

Another notion is something Davis and others refer to as the *postprandial dip*—the period, sometime after lunch and in the afternoon, when someone "just runs out of steam," as Davis says. When psychologists have studied this phenomenon, they found that fifty percent of their subjects experienced postprandial dip. The term, however, is deceptive since researchers have found that postprandial dip has nothing to do with when (or if) you have lunch. What is important to know is that one out of two persons seems to experience a postprandial dip. If you are one of them, plan and schedule your day with that afternoon energy low in mind. This is what Davis does:

> I plan around my postprandial dip. Mine is quite late—between four and five— but I know that at that time, I'd better not try to read something heavy and dull because, on the spot, it's going to put me to sleep. Living out here in New Jersey, in the summertime I go swimming between four and five because it wakes me up. In the wintertime, I use that time to go grocery shopping, since I wouldn't be able to do concentrated work anyway.

Reducing Fatigue and Stress.   Whether you're a waitress, an executive, a housewife, or a student, you will probably experience fatigue or stress at one or many points during your day or evening. This fatigue or stress may not be as predictable as your energy highs and lows, or your postprandial dip, if you experience one. Fatigue may occur because you're overworked, bored, stressed, or tired. It may occur once in a while, or at the same time each day. You may experience stress in rushing to your job in the morning, or you may lead a stressful life, feeling as if you are under stress all your waking hours, and even during your sleep.

There are numerous ways available to you to reduce stress (which will help to reduce fatigue):

> exercising (walking, calisthenics, sports activities, yoga)
> doing an optional activity that interests you
> eating well (not too much or too little)
> planning (not *over*planning)

A bank vice-president finds she has a high energy level, and less fatigue, because she is "turned on" by her work. A computer programmer never stays out after ten on work nights. A college professor, a "night person," never teaches a class before two in the afternoon. A corporate lawyer, whose average workday lasts from eight in the morning till nine at night, reduces stress and fatigue by eating lightly, jogging during her lunch hour, and taking multivitamins if she's "having a tough negotiation." A teacher who begins work at nine prefers to wake up by six, exercise, and get to school by eight. She reduces fatigue by getting to bed early, and she reduces stress by allowing ample time to get to her job. A social scientist has learned to reduce stress and fatigue by quitting work at five and rarely working on weekends, even though she does the kind of research-consulting work that could extend into every evening and weekend. "I don't stay up much past eleven anymore on weekday nights," she adds.

You may want to reduce fatigue and stress by making time in your weekly schedule for strenuous exercising as McQuade and Aikman note in *Stress.* Dr. Kenneth H. Cooper, a former Air Force medical officer, is credited with popularizing the type of exercise known as aerobics. Aerobics are strenuous activities, like running, sports activities, or even walking, done regularly. As little time as half an hour a day is said to bring positive results. The aerobics that Cooper recommends, in descending order of effectiveness, are: running, swimming, bicycle riding rapidly (about twenty miles per hour), walking (about three miles per hour), running in place, and handball, squash, or basketball.

Dr. Keith Sedlacek, director of the Stress Regulation Institute in New York and co-author of *How to Avoid Stress Before It Kills You,* describes simple activities that anyone can do—anytime and anywhere—to reduce stress and fatigue. "There are a whole series of simple muscle relaxation techniques that you can use," says Sedlacek. "Simply tensing one group of muscles, and relaxing them. There are cassette tapes, my own tapes as well as other people's, that you can play that will give you the instructions. There are also breathing exercises you can do. Fifteen minutes is usually enough time. The breathing or simple muscle exercises involve letting go of different parts of the body; it's a way of moving away from intense concentration, over-planning, and projection into the future."

There is no one way to reduce fatigue and stress that is right for everyone, just as no two persons have to manage their time in the same way. What is universally true, however, is that even if there seem to be short-term gains when you are stressed—the frenzied, competitive, success-oriented activity associated with Type A personalities—in the longer run there is less time. Less time because of temporary or prolonged burn-out or because of the diseases that have been correlated with stress, such as heart disease, as well as a shortened life span.

Setting Short-Range Priorities.   How do you apply the information that you have gathered about yourself, and how you currently manage (and want to manage) your time to improve the way you spend the rest of today, or the next six months? As noted before, long-range goals enable you to revise your daily activities so that they are steps toward achieving those goals. Long-range goals may be conceived of in broad terms—"I want to be happy," "I want to go back to work when the children are in junior high school," or in narrower ones—"I want to find a new job closer to home," "I want to reestablish my close friendship with my college roommate," or "Next year, I want to increase my commissions to forty thousand dollars." You need broad (and long-term) goals to guide you; you also need short-range priorities to facilitate achieving your long-range goals.

To assist setting short-range priorities, simplify what you want. Clarify your goals; specify your aims. This suggests that your emotions go into your goals—"I want to be a millionaire" or "I want to combine a career with raising a family"—and your intelligence goes into planning, and taking the steps, to reach those goals.

Try to simplify your goals, and set short-range priorities, by dividing your goal into a *noun* and a *verb*. Just two words. If it's more than two words, you may be the victim of muddy thinking or goal overload (wanting too many goals and probably, by wanting too many, encouraging yourself to fail at any one of them). Sometimes the verb-noun principle is clear; if you smoke, your verb-noun principle is "Quit smoking." Sometimes the verb-noun principle is cloudy; if you are dissatisfied at the office, you have to clarify your verb-noun principle to improve your situation. Is it "get a raise," "change departments," or "work shorter hours"? Once you decide on your verb-noun principle you can consider actions that will aid, or inhibit, your achievement of that goal. Whatever you do (how you spend your time) should be in the service of fulfilling your verb-noun goal.

Applying the verb-noun principle to your goals clarifies your short-range priorities.

One Day at a Time. By conceptualizing time as both short-term and long-range you will have a better chance of gaining control over it. You need long-range goals as an umbrella under which you place your short-term priorities. Those priorities have to be followed one day (step) at a time. In that way, your short-range priorities will help you actualize your long-range goals. (For some, it may be necessary to break your time down even more into "one hour at a time.")

What is your most important goal for today? If you have one, fine. If you don't, take a few moments to consider what it might be. Allow yourself only one verb-noun goal for your work and personal life. Don't overload. Accomplish those two goals and you can always add on others. Remember that to achieve your primary verb-noun goals, you will take lots of "little steps." Those steps are not goals; they are the steps to accomplish your goals.

In the next chapter, time wasters that inhibit you from accomplishing your "verb-noun principle" will be explored. You will note in that chapter, as well as in the chapters that follow, that interruptions may inhibit you from attaining your goals. You have to learn to discriminate between unnecessary interruptions and new demands that are short-term priorities. It's unrealistic to think that you can just work toward your verb-noun goal and nothing else. Deciding what is busywork, a distraction, or a short-term priority is the main difference between frenzied and effective time managers. Learn the consequences of postponing, as well as deciding which deadlines are fixed, and which ones are negotiable.

To help you set short-range priorities for your goals, and to learn to set aside time for unforeseen short-range priorities, use the space below to plan how you will take control of your time tomorrow:

Date _____

CAREER GOAL: *Verb* _____   *Noun* _____
Short-range priorities (steps) related to achieving that goal:

1. _____

2. _____

3. _____

Other short-range priorities (now known, or fill in as they occur):

4. _____

5. _____

6. _____

PERSONAL GOAL: *Verb* _____   *Noun* _____
Short-range priorities (steps) related to achieving that goal:

1. _____

2. _____

3. _____

Other short-range priorities (now known, or fill in as they occur):

4. _____

5. _____

6. _____

Think of your time as a series of activities or tasks to be completed, sometimes structured around the arbitrary distinctions known as minutes, hours, days, or even years. Those time divisions should be in the service of your short-range priorities and long-term goals. Now go back over the work sheets you just created and consider: "How long will this take?" At this stage, your estimates may be more ideal than real. (You probably *under*estimate how long something takes. Add on at least ten percent to your estimate so you come out on time.)

In setting priorities, planning, and scheduling, you might also remember the principle of the nineteenth-century Italian economist and sociologist Vilfredo Pareto, Pareto's 80/20 Principle: About 20 percent of what you do will give you 80 percent of your results. Examples: 20 percent of your house will get 80 percent of the dirt; 20 percent of the people using customer services will give you 80 percent of the headaches; 20 percent of your research will get you 80 percent of your report. Going after the "right" 20 percent will get you 80 percent of your results. *In other words, doing the right thing as best you can is more effective than doing the wrong thing magnificently.*

The more effectively you conquer the time wasters discussed in the next chapter, the more accurate your predictions will be about how long it will take to accomplish that 20 percent (the steps that are the best use of your time). Identifying that 20 percent, and being effective, may mean the difference between pleasing your boss or inspiring wrath, or even getting your income tax return in on time this year. By creatively managing your work and personal time, you will become more effective, productive, and self-satisfied.

TERMS

time management	workaholism
A B C approach	time log
burn-out	postprandial dip
verb-noun principle	fatigue
stress	Pareto's 80/20 Principle

REFERENCES

BOLLES, RICHARD NELSON. *What Color Is Your Parachute?* Berkeley, Calif.: Ten Speed Press, 1978, 1972. A job hunting and career changing guide; see especially Chapter 5 on setting goals (career and life planning).

DAVIS, FLORA. *Living Alive!* Garden City, N.Y.: Doubleday, 1980.

DOUGLASS, MERRILL E., and DONNA N. DOUGLASS. *Manage Your Time, Manage Your Work, Manage Yourself.* New York: AMACOM, a division of American Management Association, 1980.

FREUDENBERGER, HERBERT J., with GERALDINE RICHELSON. *Burn-Out: The High Cost of High Achievement.* Garden City, N.Y.: Doubleday & Company, Inc., 1980. Psychoanalyst Freudenberger thinks one need not be neurotic or psychotic to experience burn-out symptoms—a loss of meaning to life; an inability to get along with family, friends, and co-workers; disillusionment; frustration; and the necessity of increasing amounts of energy to continue the fast pace one has set for oneself.

HALL, EDWARD T. *The Dance of Life: The Other Dimension of Time.* Garden City, N.Y.: Anchor Press/Doubleday, 1983.

LAKEIN, ALAN. *How to Get Control of Your Time and Your Life.* New York: New American Library, 1973. Lakein summarizes his best-known tips, including "If a thing is worth doing, it's worth doing badly!"

MACKENZIE, ALEC, and KAY CHRONKITE WALDO. *About Time!* New York: McGraw-Hill Book Company, 1981.

MCQUADE, WALTER, and ANN AIKMAN. *Stress.* New York: Bantam Books, 1975. An easy-to-read and thorough book for the layperson on what stress can do to you, how stress occurs, and how to reduce it.

RUTHERFORD, ROBERT D. *Just In Time.* New York: John Wiley & Sons, 1981.

SEDLACEK, KEITH, and MATTHEW CULLIGAN. *How to Avoid Stress Before It Kills You.* New York: Gramercy Press, Crown Books, 1979.

ZERUBAVEL, EVIATAR. *Hidden Rhythms: Schedules and Calendars in Social Life.* Chicago: The University of Chicago Press, 1981.

EXERCISES

1. Apply Pareto's 80/20 Principle to a specific task you must do—writing a monthly report, planning a conference, cleaning the house, etc. Figure out which 20 percent of the tasks you would do will result in 80 percent of your end result. Prune down your efforts to match those high payoff activities.

2. Fill in additional time logs for yourself for one work or school day, and one leisure day. Are there times when you waste your time? Are there times when you seem to be more productive? Think about how you feel during various parts of each day. Are there hours when you are more tired or more alert than other hours? Is that the time when you are also most productive, or are you doing something that fails to use your natural energy levels fully?

3. On a blank time log, or a blank sheet of paper, create an "ideal" workday or leisure day that you would like to follow. Keep it simple, but be sure to include such important parts of your ideal day as exercising, time with friends, spouse, or children, reading, etc. Post your ideal day in a prominent place and study it, so that you can work toward that goal.

4. Do you know one or more individuals who seem to manage their time effectively and efficiently? Talk with them to find out how they do it.

2
Obstacles to Effective Time Management

Procrastination is the thief of time.

EDWARD YOUNG
(*Night Thoughts*)

TIME WASTERS

Do you ever feel as if you're wasting time? If you know about common time wasters, you'll be better equipped to guard against them. This chapter will describe the following time traps, and offer solutions for overcoming them:

- Doing too much at once
- The inability to say "no"
- Procrastination
- Complaining
- Fear of failure
- Fear of success
- Devaluing (or overvaluing) your work/personal activities
- Perfectionism
- Impatience and low frustration tolerance
- Being in love, and other emotional afflictions
- Jealousy
- The inability to take criticism
- Commuting and travel time
- The terrible twos: telephone and television
- Bad habits

Even if you think you need help with only a few of the fifteen time wasters listed above, consider reading this entire chapter. You may be surprised to recognize more time wasting habits in yourself than you expected.

Doing Too Much At Once

"Call on me for help any time, Joe."

You want to redecorate your home, read a novel, buy a pair of shoes, call a friend who's in the hospital, rewrite a memo, and make the final preparations for a business trip. Which activity do you do first? How many commitments can you take on without impairing the quality of the results? When are you overloading yourself, and when are you operating efficiently?

Rule of thumb: If you think *you have too many things to do, you're probably right.*

You know your situations, your capacities, and your limitations best. At one point in your life— say, when you're in high school— you might be able to handle more leisure activities than later, when you're married, with two growing children, working at a full-time job. You can handle as many different tasks as you like, as long as you don't feel you're trying to do too much in the allotted time. As one woman put it, "I take on so much that all of a sudden I just feel panicked, and I start screwing everything up."

Learning not to do too much at once involves two issues: (1) doing fewer things at any one time; and (2) doing one thing "at a time."

This "concentrating on one thing at a time" principle applies to studying French, preparing dinner, listening to a friend, reading a book, or anything else. You give that activity your all before getting involved in something else. Your concentration is on that one task. The length of that concentration is up to you, but during that activity, you are completely and totally involved in it. Example: Lawyers may "work on" matters for twenty clients a week, but since cases and projects are in varying stages of completion—from a planning meeting to drawing up a contract or getting ready to appear in court— rarely is the lawyer actually working on more than one thing at any one moment. Yet in one day, he may give some time to almost all of them! And do it effectively.

Obviously, we all have much to do during any given hour, day, or week. Doing one thing at a time ensures that major commitments are kept under control. You don't learn to scuba dive and ice skate at the same time, but you do concurrently see friends, perform at work, and take care of your home. We are all guilty of trying to do too many things at once, to a greater or lesser degree. Often, in attempting too much at once, less is accomplished than desired, and it may take longer or be of lesser quality.

Ask yourself if you do too much at once because you need the thrill of getting involved in new projects and obligations, but find—because of a fear of success, a fear of failure, perfectionism, or procrastination—that you take on new tasks before you have completed the old ones. If you have that tendency, you will have to recognize it, understand it, and force yourself to finish obligations before you begin new ones. For you, the thrill of being asked is so powerful that you miscalculate how much time it will take, and what is involved.

Remember: It takes more time, and it is harder, to finish most tasks than to start them. Completing tasks before starting new ones will help you to limit how many things you do at once.

If you are prone to the "doing too much at once" syndrome, try to set priorities, and stick to them. Decide what task you will do first, second, and third. Try making a list of things to do, rating each item by importance—1, 2, 3 or A, B, C. Then force yourself to complete number 1, or A. You might consider creating your own "Things to Do" sheets, or buying them in pads. (See Chapter Three, "Becoming Organized," for guidelines on formulating, and using, lists of Things to Do.) R. James Steffen, author of *How Outstanding People Manage Time,* calls this M.I.N. (*Most Important Now*). Dru Scott, author of *How to Put More Time In Your Life,* expresses the same concept in this way: "Clarify priorities for yourself and others." The increased time that you productively spend on your priority project may astound you. Ironically, this focused approach will result in accomplishing more projects—one at a time—than you would achieve by doing too many things at once.

If you need variety in what you do, rather than sticking to only one job until it is completed, consider the time-effective way that Isaac Asimov, author of more than 280 books, copes with that. He has four major projects that he works on "at once," but when he is working on any one of those four projects, that one project—whatever stage it is in—has his full attention. (For some, however, shifting gears and starting up on new projects wastes their time. A strict one-project-at-a-time-from-start-to-finish rule may be what's needed.)

In summary, to overcome your "doing too much at once" syndrome, *prioritize,* creating clear, specific goals for each day, and each hour (or period) of the day, accomplishing each goal or task before going on to the next one. Decide which tasks require your exclusive attention and which ones you can do simultaneously. You can listen to the radio while driving your car, but you can't read the newspaper. You can read the newspaper while working out on a stationary bicycle, but you probably couldn't work on your report while exercising.

The Inability to Say "No"

"As long as you're going out for the mail, could you pick up the laundry and get a few things at the store?"

Quite often, behind the "doing too many things at once" syndrome is someone who can't say "no." Saying "yes" when you should say "no" arises from the childish wish to please everyone, and represents a failure to adequately define what's important to you. It's hard to say "no." You may fear an opportunity will never come again, or that saying "no" will hurt someone's feelings forever.

Saying "no"—gracefully—is a two-step process. You decide what your needs and limits are, and then you say "no" to whatever interferes. You are saying "no" because whatever is asked of you is not the best use of *your* time. How convincing you are (and the acceptance of the "no") is generally a function of how well you've convinced yourself. You and your wife have just decided to go out to dinner on Saturday night when the phone rings, and you're asked to visit friends who live two hours away. Say "no," and briefly note that you have other plans. It's not the fact that you're saying "no" that can alienate someone, but how you express yourself. Tell the truth, express your gratitude for the invitation and, if appropriate, suggest another time to get together.

What do you do if you can't say "no"? Write the word in big letters by your telephone or on the desk where you answer your mail. Don't be wishy-washy and say "maybe"; a tactful "no" is what's needed.

Lynn Diamond, founder and president of Innovative Information Techniques, a time management consulting firm based in New York, has sound advice to those who have an inability to say no:

> The first thing one has to do is to really think: Do you mean *yes*, or do you mean *no*? If you're not clear in your *own* mind, you're not going to communicate that, just as you can't be half pregnant. The second thing in saying *no* is to remember that the person who made the request has a need. At the moment that they ask you to do something, you are their solution. To say *no* and not to help them solve their problem is a monumental turn-off. You are not likely to be seen as an integral part of the business, or to get new assignments. The real thing in saying *no* is to help generate options. How can you help that person to solve the problem? You might mean, "No, not now" or "No, not me." Thirdly, you have to be realistic; sometimes you can't afford to say *no*. However, if you say *yes* to get out of a situation, but fail to perform, you lose your credibility and you become a person another person can't depend upon.

Diamond's "No, not now" and "No, not me" advice is clear. However, in a culture like ours, where "It's now or never" seems to be the programmed expectation, "No, not now" may take a little convincing on your part. Example: you want to start a discussion group but you currently have too many other commitments. You tell your friend "No, not now," but you keep in touch, assuring her the time will come. Almost a year and several fulfilled commitments later, you and your friend meet, make the necessary arrangements, and the first meeting of the discussion group takes place. Your "No, not now" became a "yes," validating the original "no."

When you do mean "No, never," you can reject the request without dismissing the person asking it. Too often someone with a problem of saying "no" gracefully turns against the person who makes the demand. (A variation on the "blame the messenger for the bad news" philosophy.)

You should also consider adding to "No, not now" and "No, not me" a third component, namely, "No, not this." "No, not this" is a good time saver because it enables you to turn almost any "no" situation into an opportunity. Example: after a job interview, you decide this is not the right job for you. How you handle "No, not this" may mean the difference between wasting the interviewer's time (and yours) and turning it into a future opportunity. (You may want to impress her so that she someday considers you for a job that *is* for you. You may want to ensure a positive report about you to the referral or employment agency, who will then try even harder to work on your behalf.) The situations to which "No, not this" applies are innumerable. Creatively handling "No, not this" encounters will enable you to turn chances that are less than ideal into options.

Procrastination

"I'll take care of it tomorrow—or by Thursday at the latest."

Procrastination means doing one thing—perhaps something pleasant—when you should be doing something else—an obligation. Examples: watching TV instead of repairing the broken toaster; rearranging the magazines instead of reading them; putting off a term paper for four months only to start it the night before it's due.

The very act of delay can have consequences; if a couple delays making a decision about having a family, it may be "too late" by the time they do decide to have a child. If you wait so long before you start a project that you lack adequate time to do a good job on it, you've given yourself a less than optimal chance to succeed.

In *Overcoming Procrastination,* psychologists Albert Ellis and William J. Knaus list these main causes of procrastination: self-downing [putting oneself down] (anxiety and depression); low frustration tolerance (depression and hopelessness); and hostility (anger and resentment). To their list I would add fear of success, fear of failure, and almost every other time waster discussed in this chapter.

Five solutions to procrastinating will be discussed in the pages that follow, including: (1) Developing a procrastination list so you can pinpoint when you are procrastinating, and the consequences; (2) Making the priority task that you are procrastinating about the first job of the day; (3) The reward system; (4) Learning how to be a "creative" procrastinator; and (5) Allowing for delays.

To help you to overcome your tendency to procrastinate, understand what you do when you are procrastinating, and the consequences of those actions. (Some people are so busy doing "other things" that they fail to realize that they are procrastinating about doing what they really need to do.) Take a sheet of paper and write down some of the activities that you engage in when procrastinating about completing (or starting) some all-important task.

If you have trouble knowing that you are procrastinating, consider one woman's way of reminding herself that she's putting something off. Roberta, a legal secretary, knows she has a problem with procrastination. Every Monday morning, she checks her calendar; any tasks she failed to do the week before are rewritten for the current Monday, for her to do in the coming week. She finds that some tasks are moved weekly—for months—until she finally gets around to doing them. A variation on that theme is to have a short list of the one, two, or more essential tasks that you must do. Until you can cross an item off your "priority" list, you have a visual reminder that you are procrastinating.

A procedure that many have found "cures" a tendency toward procrastination—long enough to accomplish the priority task at hand—is to make that priority task the very first thing tackled that day. Example: Carol, 28, a middle manager in a foreign bank, was unable to complete her Master's thesis. Finally, since she had a full-time job, she started getting up each morning at 4:30 and, until 7:30, she sat at the typewriter—whether or not she was able to get anything done. After a while, she did start writing instead of just staring.

You might also try the reward system to lick your procrastination problem. Decide in advance what reward you'll give yourself if you start and stay with a necessary but unpleasant task.

Write down the task you have to do:

To do: _____

Now decide on what you will reward yourself with after it's done:

My reward will be: _____

Make sure the reward that you decide on is something you truly enjoy so you'll have the motivation to keep at your necessary task. Just a few possibilities are: giving a party; going to a movie; talking on the phone; buying a new outfit; or relaxing for an hour.

Another solution to procrastination is what I call creative procrastination. It's creative because it helps you to achieve your overall goal by reordering short-term priorities (or steps) so that energy-sapping "blocks" are avoided. Although you temporarily avoid one unpleasant task by replacing it with a pleasant one, you discipline yourself to choose a pleasant one related to your overall goal. For example, you have to write up a report and you've reached a point where you find yourself putting it off and getting involved in distractions and less important things, like talking on the phone or watching TV. (Unfortunately some other "things," like starting another report, may generate more tasks, and related activities, that get you committed to tasks that you may, again, procrastinate about accomplishing.) Instead of procrastinating by making a call to a friend—and not really enjoying the conversation because you feel guilty about procrastinating—you accomplish tasks related to your number one project. Let's say your report requires a bibliography. Instead of calling your friend when you are blocked on writing the report, you work on the report's bibliography. Another example: you have correspondence to do and you're procrastinating so you address the envelopes, or gather together the necessary materials to write the letters, rather than switch to another unrelated task.

Creative procrastination allows you to deviate from your ideal of working sequentially, from task to task, until you're done, but you may get the job done in the same, or even less, time. This method requires flexibility in your approach to your tasks (and it may not work in all situations), but for projects comprised of numerous steps it can help you to conquer a seeming insurmountable tendency to delay.

Another solution to procrastination is to "allow" yourself to procrastinate. Like all solutions you have to be careful that this does not get out of hand so that you permanently avoid an unpleasant task. Sometimes just an hour, a day, or a week away from the task you are procrastinating about will provide the necessary energy, and motivation, to go forward with that task. (You may also find that an external motivation occurs to prompt you along: "The moving men are coming in two days" can inspire you to finish the packing you put off for two months.)

Procrastination may be tied to perfectionism in that you want, or need, to perform in a way that conforms to an unrealistic standard of excellence. Giving yourself permission to "goof off" or have a period of controlled procrastination may help you deal with this common problem without guilt or self-downing. "I'll call to cancel my reservation after I read this newspaper article" is more efficient than putting off the phone call for days at a time, spending more time reminding yourself to do it than the time spent on the phone.

The worst thing procrastinators can do is to abandon an important goal, or task, because they feel too embarrassed, discouraged, or guilty to finally tackle (and finish) a long-avoided activity. Usually "better never than late" does not apply. You reap the benefits of licking procrastination, just as you pay the most for failing to overcome it.

In some situations, however, delay is necessary or beneficial—e.g., planning something before doing it, completing your most important goal before your secondary ones. The trick is to know the difference between effective and self-indulgent procrastination.

Complaining

"And then I had to wait twenty minutes for him to fix the copier, and then . . ."

How often have you uttered a complaint, and immediately wished you hadn't? Our culture sanctions silent stoicism, with phrases like "stiff upper lip," and "never complain, never explain." Yet, the act of complaining is natural, and quite prevalent. Its legitimacy is judged by: what you gripe about; to whom you bleat; and how often you grumble.

These three criteria interrelate; together, they determine whether a statement is deemed an observation, a self-pitying complaint, or a time waster. For example, getting your gripes off your chest once in a while might help you break through your delaying tactics. Complaining might provide you with information; e.g., you complain to a co-worker about the deadline pressures you feel and she tells you the proposal isn't due for another month.

If your complaint is about a specific person—and you can't go forward until your differences are resolved—a face-to-face confrontation might be the most efficient way to handle things. If that is unrealistic, writing a long letter—one that you might ultimately decide would be best unmailed—can "get it all out" and help you go on with the business at hand. (A daily journal serves the same purpose, but on an ongoing basis.)

By and large, chronic complaining wastes time that could be spent thinking and doing. Complaints can bring strangers and intimates closer—or send them running for cover. Hilda, 68, a retired librarian, says, "Complaining is probably good fc. the person who complains, and awful for everyone else around."

Complaining may be a way to gain sympathy or control in a situation. Example: "I worked like a dog today. On the floor for five hours trying to fix the equipment and you think *you* have problems?" The man who said that to his wife did not want to listen to her. His complaints may have been his way of justifying why she should be spending her time catering to his needs, and not vice versa.

Complaining not only wastes your own time, but also creates a very poor image of what you're like—people will welcome your sympathy yet will make a mental note that you cannot be relied on for "positive thinking." You may find the label "Gloomy Gus" a difficult one to live down.

Solutions: Listen more to what others say and you may realize your complaints are petty. Read some books, like Harold S. Kushner's *When Bad*

Things Happen to Good People or Viktor E. Frankl's *Man's Search for Meaning,* and consider ways other than complaining that you might try to get through life's disappointments. A thirty-seven-year old bachelor, for example, does volunteer work with terminally ill cancer patients rather than complaining about his own loneliness. Accent the positive in life, and be more realistic in expectations, so you'll have less to complain about. One chronic complainer confesses, "Even if I go way beyond my goals I am still not satisfied." Ask yourself: Do I complain because I have nothing else to say? If your answer is "yes," make sure you read the section on compulsive talking later on in this book. Do you complain to get attention? If so, find more effective attention-getting mechanisms, such as increasing your knowledge in a certain area so you have more to say, or looking more attractive. Plan, and execute, actions that may correct specific complaints that now preoccupy you. Speak your complaints into a tape recorder and force yourself to listen to the tape, as if you were the co-worker, friend, or spouse who might have to listen to *you.* If all else fails, complain to taxi drivers, bartenders, or therapists who expect to hear complaints as part of their job.

Fear of Failure

"What if it explodes when we turn it on, Orville?"

If you don't try, you can't fail. By working at a level far below your potential, you never have to worry about taking the risks involved in giving your all— whether to a project, a relationship, or a job.

The causes of a fear of failure, a fear that wastes time by inhibiting action, are the same as the causes of stage fright, described in *The Secret of Charisma* by actress Doe Lang, president of Charismedia, Inc.:

1. Fear of not doing as well as you want to.
2. Insufficient or inadequate preparation.
3. Fear of what people (the audience) will think.
4. Earlier negative experiences.
5. Inadequate enjoyment of what you're doing (probably due to 1, 2, 3, or 4).

You can do something about all the above causes except number 4, earlier negative experiences. The best you can do about earlier negative experiences is to understand them, and to refuse to fail because of them. All the other causes of a fear of failure may be reduced or eliminated by doing all that you can to insure your success. Adequate training and experience will aid you. *Confidence, which reduces a fear of failure, comes from competence and accomplishment.*

Example: If you have to deliver a lecture, spend adequate time preparing it, rehearsing it, making any necessary note cards for yourself, and selecting what you'll wear; allow adequate time to get to your meeting.

Another way to conquer your fear of failure is to reevaluate how you view failure. Making mistakes (failure) has a negative connotation in our culture; we applaud achievement and push thwarted relationships or projects under the rug. Without those "failures," (it's better to call them "efforts"), there could be no successes. Susan, 34, an actress who has had more jobs as a waitress than parts in plays, describes her fear of failing as an actress: "I wonder if all the time that I thought I was good, and thought I was talented, maybe it wasn't really true. That would mean that I would have to change my whole life, change my career. I would have to have a whole new life, and that's very frightening."

Once Susan, and others who fear failure, analyze the situation that they fear, they may open up new options (and successes) for themselves. Overcoming a fear of failure means interpreting every mistake the way corporate consultant and management professor Peter F. Drucker does. Writing in *The Practice of Management,* he states "... Nobody learns except by making mistakes. The better a man is the more mistakes he will make—for the more new things he will try. I would never promote a man into a top-level job who has not made mistakes, and big ones at that. Otherwise he is sure to be mediocre. Worse still, not having made mistakes he will not have learned how to spot them early and how to correct them."

Failure itself is not fatal; fearing it can be. Another way to cope with a fear of failure is to imagine the worst consequences of what you are doing. Take the failure you fear and fantasize it to the extreme. Example: you overcome your fear of failure and give up your middle management job to go back to school and become an accountant. You graduate, become licensed, but cannot get a job. Or you cannot get clients. Or you decide, after all that, that you really liked the job you left better than being an accountant. Ask yourself: Can you live with that? Could you still view the years of study as useful even if you go back to your old job? *By imagining the worst that might happen, and picturing yourself overcoming that failure, you can go on to try the goals you fear.*

Fear of failure is tied very closely to fear of success. The solution for a fear of failure is similar to the solution for a fear of success: do your best but if you fail learn what you can from what you did (or did not) do. Each experience increases your ability to withstand further failures (mistakes). A tip: if you find yourself blaming everyone else or circumstances each time you fail, your fear of failure may be causing you to waste time by avoiding responsibility. Objective self-evaluation, unlike "if only" fantasies, saves time by using mistakes creatively for self-advancement.

Fear of Success

"Will God be angry if it works, Wilbur?"

No one wants to fail, and everyone wants to succeed, right? Wrong. According to psychologist Leon Tec and others, a fear of success is quite common. In *Fear of Success* Tec writes: "I believe the fear of success is universal, so widespread that it must be considered normal. It may be severe in some people, less intense in others, but it is always there. Even for those who ostensibly have succeeded and reached the top of their fields, the fear of success may exist and rob them of the enjoyment of their feats."

Take a few moments to fantasize about what would happen if you were successful—really successful—in either your professional or personal life. Would friends or relatives be jealous? What would you do differently? Would you squander your fortune, or become addicted to drugs? Will the old gang feel you're not one of them anymore? Would you become depressed because you would have nothing left to strive for? Strange as it sounds, some people grow used to being unhappy—or poor or fat or lonely. Susan, the struggling actress, says, "There's something secure in staying where you are, no matter how bad it is, rather than going into something else, unknown ground."

Psychologist Carol Lindemann of the Phobia Division of the New York Psychological Center describes a typical fear of success syndrome:

> Fear of success results from underlying anxieties and ambivalences behind avoidance of certain tasks. Let's say that a young woman is raised to do something in her life that is better than what her parents have done. She finishes college, gets a Master's degree, and all of a sudden she is faced with setting out in the world. Suddenly she panics, literally or within herself, about the fearsome kinds of steps that she has to take. She fears that her inadequacies will prevent her from achieving the formula for success that has been laid out for her. She may start to withdraw, eventually becoming housebound, not doing anything. The treatment here is to bring her ideal of success down to manageable proportions; something that really can be achieved. The question is, "What are the anxieties which would be raised if I were to make it?" By understanding those anxieties, you are half way toward sorting it through. You then have a choice. You can resolve the conflict in a conscious way, not by neurotically acting it out, letting the fear direct your life.

Try this to face up to your fear of success: imagine the best that could happen—and all the negative consequences that might follow—and see yourself coping with that. Picture yourself coping with the joys success will bring, as well as the disappointments.

Ask yourself how realistic are your images of success. Is it all rosy and wonderful? If you fantasize success as only positive you may be afraid to succeed and negate your unrealistic expectations. Consider that success may mean that you, and everyone else, may expect more from you in the future. You may be afraid of the good, and bad, changes that success will necessitate. Is success your "if only . . ." one-note song that camouflages deep-seated insecurity? Are your standards so high, and so unrealistic, that you are successful, and you don't even know it? Thus you may have to become more realistic about what success means—at work and in personal relationships— to discover if you have achieved it and, if not, how to go about getting it.

Devaluing (or Overvaluing) of Your Work/Personal Activities

> "Knock knock."
> "Who's there?"
> "It's only me."

For some, it's difficult to believe—and live up to the belief—that what they do matters. "In the end it doesn't really matter what you do," says a man with low self-esteem. There are also those who are so self-important that they think their every deed is momentous. ("Look at me," they seem to be saying, as if the whole world is one big parent whose love they are trying to win.) Then there are those who waver back and forth between these two extremes— either it's the best or the worst. Dealing with life realistically means operating somewhere in the middle. It is a waste of time to be either a minimizer or a maximizer; both are distorted views of events and persons. It's also hard to expect those around you to share your intense interest in what Tom Wolfe described as "that most fascinating of all subjects: me."

A solution to devaluing, or overvaluing, your work or personal activities is to honestly appraise your past efforts, your current time demands, and your future goals. Are your paintings good enough to show in a gallery, or are they second-rate by artistic standards but first-rate as a hobby? Is the report you wrote terrific, or just "so-so," and not something you should be bragging about? As a friend used to say, when asked what she thought about a new date, "Good, not great." Most efforts fall into the "good, not great" category. Perceiving everything you do as worthless or, the opposite extreme, brilliant, is a time waster.

Perfectionism

> "Just a little more to the left.
> A little further.
> No, back to the right . . ."

The perfectionist is never pleased and, sometimes without knowing it, belabors assignments, and reworks things past deadlines. Perfectionism is a difficult habit to break because it means rethinking one's entire approach to how one appraises people, things, and events. We all need ideals to aspire to, but when the ideal becomes a day-to-day goal, frustration and poor time management can result. Why try at all if your efforts will never satisfy you or anyone else? Or so thinks the perfectionist.

Sometimes those who are overweight are really perfectionists about their appearance. Overweight, they can fantasize about how perfect they'd be if they lost weight. Afraid to test out their hypothesis, they live in a world of frustration, with time and energy wasted in fear, regrets, or dissatisfaction. Sometimes those looking for the perfect mate fail to find a mate at all. The only cure for perfectionism is realism. Once you face this problem, you can begin to recognize when you're defeating yourself by setting goals which are out of reach. Are you a perfectionist? You may not be a perfectionist about everything, just certain things. You may be a perfectionist about others, always finding fault and wishing they dressed, spoke, acted, or went about their lives in a different ("perfect") way. Perfectionists have a low self-image concealed behind their "I know what's right" facade.

Perfectionism is an extreme character trait that interferes with effective use of your time. (Some degree of perfectionism is time-effective, but that is when you strive for excellence, not perfection.) Perfectionism camouflages fear of failure and of success. You're so afraid of failing that you set standards inappropriate to the task—for example, you spend four days over the one-paragraph letter you have to do, writing and rewriting beyond realistic standards of excellence. You're so afraid of succeeding that you convince yourself your letter is still not good enough so you never send it or you send it thinking you could have—should have—done better.

What you want to do, if you have this trait in one or more areas, is to turn your perfectionism into something more manageable and useful to you. By becoming more realistic in your expectations, perfectionism can be converted into high, but attainable, standards. A possible solution for the perfectionist is to delegate authority. By accepting that someone can do certain jobs for you—perhaps not as well but as well as the task requires—you will free up valuable time and energy for other pursuits. (The time you save by not vacuuming the rug a second time that week you might use to read a book, do volunteer work, socialize, or simply relax.)

Becoming more accepting of your strengths, and weaknesses, is the first step toward a more relaxed approach to yourself, your work, and to others. Thus a solution to perfectionism is to become aware of what you miss because of your perfectionism. It may, interestingly, be in only one or a few areas that you, or someone you know, is a perfectionist. Parents may have such unrealistic standards for their children that their offspring can never please them (or themselves). Everyone misses out on enjoying what reality is by focusing on perfectionistic fantasies.

In summary, here are specific solutions for perfectionism:

(1) Develop more realistic assessments of yourself, others, and situations.
(2) Realize that no one—nothing—is perfect.
(3) Become more flexible by accepting that there are more than two ways to do something (your way, and the wrong way).
(4) If your perfectionism is a way of preventing yourself from feeling good about yourself or what you do, learn to feel comfortable being complimented.
(5) Turn perfectionism into high but realistic standards by evaluating how perfectionism wastes your time and others'. (Should you send out that letter with one corrected misspelling, or spend half an hour retyping it?)

Impatience and Low Frustration Tolerance

"Would you hurry up and finish that symphony, Ludwig?"

Are you impatient? Impatience prevents optimal use of your time. Examples: you're so eager to complete one phone call, and get on to the next, that you fail to be a good listener or to remember much of what was said. Difficulty in handling frustration is related to impatience. That wastes time because your energy is spent fuming at problems—not solving them. Both these "I want it now" personality traits are time wasters in the same way that perfectionism wastes time. Impatience may cause you to give up before you have expended the time and effort needed for the task at hand; perfectionism may cause you to redo or prolong a task too long because your standards are too high. Those who are impatient, and have low frustration tolerance, are filled with self-loathing, since they give up too quickly to see the results that they crave; those who are perfectionists are usually too hard on themselves (and others) and won't give up even when they have done as much as necessary or feasible.

Like other time wasters, retraining yourself to be less impatient, and to have a higher frustration tolerance, in one area of your life may help you to successfully apply it, step by step, to other areas as well. Pick a task to complete, or a bad habit that you want to change, and force yourself to stick with your goal in spite of impatience or low frustration tolerance. That specific instance of conquering impatience may help you to generalize your overall approach to your activities and relationships. Look at impatience and low frustration tolerance as phobias and cure those tendencies in the way you would treat a phobic response to, let's say, an elevator. You get in the elevator and don't close the doors. Then you get into the elevator and ride to the fourth floor. In time, you are able to ride to the top of the World Trade Center with a carload of people and still feel comfortable. Start off sticking to a task that requires some patience; finishing that task even when you become frustrated will enable you to go on to a task that requires more patience.

Impatience and low frustration tolerance are symptomatic of immaturity and a need for immediate gratification. Yet many of the greatest rewards in how we spend our time are for accomplishing little steps and continuing on a path even when frustrated. Curing impatience and low frustration tolerance means becoming process-, not product-, oriented. You may want to appear on national television hyping your best-selling novel, but you won't get there unless you are willing to find more private daily rewards in the day-to-day efforts necessary to achieve that goal.

You may also have to learn how to handle the impatience of others if you are to handle your time more effectively. If you believe in the path you have chosen, even if it means being patient about monetary or other gratifications, it may require convincing those around you that they have to be more patient.

The next time something happens that demonstrates that you are impatient or that you have a low frustration tolerance—your new video recorder breaks down and you scream at the store owner, for example—decide that you have the self-control necessary to handle that frustration in a more patient, mature way. Practicing patience is reinforcing.

Being in Love, and Other Emotional Afflictions

You thought you would be able to pull yourself together during your annual vacation. Yet you are back at work, still preoccupied with your problems. Job counselors, psychologists, and psychiatrists with whom I spoke agreed that personal crises should not be resolved at work or at school. Yet many workers or students ask colleagues, classmates, employers, or professors for sympathy or advice. Why? "They want their problems remedied," says New York psychologist Joan Freyberg. She finds that more commonly women talk out personal problems with co-workers and supervisors. "They are looking for solutions. But work is a competitive situation and being too open about personal problems may be seen as a weakness that is eventually used against you."

Evaluate your current productivity and ask yourself if personal relationships or affairs are affecting how you manage your time. If you are being productive, no one, including you, should have to consider this issue any further. But if being in love or personal problems are preventing you from doing your best, you have some decisions to make. Your goal is to solve your problems, of course, but, along the way, to do well enough at your job that you don't lose it while you put your affairs back in order. Should you tell your boss or your instructor the reason your productivity is lower? "You have to show as much discretion in that decision as you do in any other," says Stanley N. Cohen, a Portland, Oregon marriage and family therapist, who is also Director of Technical Assistance for the Association of Family Conciliation Courts. Cohen suggests getting help from a conciliation service or a private therapist, if, for example, you find you're bringing your problems to work or to school. Short-term therapy of three to five sessions might help. Unlike long-term therapy, it's directed at a specific situation: "Here's what happened to me. Here's what I want to be able to do. Can you help me?"

Here are some symptoms that your personal problems are affecting your work or school performance:

- Your concentration is poor.
- Your sense of time is distorted; the hours drag on.
- Your personal problems preoccupy you at work.
- You begin to "look" busy while you're working or studying, but you are only shuffling papers and not accomplishing anything.
- You personalize everything that happens. ("He doesn't like my report because he's trying to undermine my success." "She put through that call because she's angry at me today.")

Not everyone needs outside professional help to cope with personal problems. A support network of friends is invaluable in getting you through the crisis without inappropriately relying on co-workers or superiors. If you think just getting time away from work will help, should you tell your co-workers, superiors, or subordinates the real reason you need it? The experts' consensus is: Physical complaints ("I think I'm coming down with a cold") are more acceptable, and carry less of a stigma, than tales of emotional duress.

You may also find that the opposite situation is true—your love and personal life are fine but your efforts at work or school leave something to be desired. Somehow—on your own, with the aid of friends, or with the help of a therapist—you have to find a way to improve the situation that displeases you without destroying the ones that are okay. If you chronically bring problems home from the office, you may find your dutiful listeners no longer there. Refer back to the section in this chapter on complaining, and concentrate your efforts on improving the faulty situation.

Jealousy

"If I had his connections, I'd be a vice-president too."

Jealousy is a time waster because it fosters downing others (and yourself) instead of doing whatever it takes to get what you want. "Jealousy gets the upper hand at times when we're least secure and solid within ourselves," Colette Dowling writes in *The Cinderella Complex*. Her book is an in-depth study of dependent women but her insight about jealousy applies to everyone.

Learn to recognize jealousy in yourself and in others even when it is disguised. "I don't care if she makes seventy-five thousand dollars, she'll still be miserable" or "How lucky he is to have a loving wife" are wet-blanket statements that attempt to diminish an accomplishment (and perpetuate the jealousy of the speaker).

You cannot stop others from being jealous of you, although you may wish to reevaluate why you seem to surround yourself with jealous people. You can, however, learn to understand, and minimize, the jealousy that you feel, and that wastes your time. A solution for your own time-sapping jealousy is to turn it into something positive and productive. Jealousy pinpoints what you value, since the rage and envy you feel when someone else achieves something clarifies what you want for yourself. Turn your jealousy into a fact-finding expedition; find out how he did what he did and try to learn from that how you can do it too. Put your fantasies of "if only" to the test and see if there is information to be gained that would save you time, and help you to achieve what you really want. Become secure enough within yourself that you do not need to diminish others through feeling, or expressing, jealousy. Take the time and energy that you used to spend being jealous and work at achieving what you want, whether that is wealth, fame, popularity, confidence, a nicer disposition, greater productivity, or whatever your pleasure.

The Inability to Take Criticism

"Are you saying I have lousy grammer?"

This is an incredible time waster since it may lead to abandoning a project because one small part has to be changed, to counterproductive self-hate, and to poor relationships, since those who are unable to take criticism often blame, and may actually hate, the ones who criticize them. You have to learn how to deal with criticism in an objective way if you are to make better use of your time.

"Sometimes I can feel so devastated by criticism that I feel that I want to give up acting," says Susan, the aspiring actress who also has a fear of failure. Interestingly, Susan is only "devastated" if the criticism is from someone she "respects." "Some people I just don't respect," she says, "so the criticism means absolutely nothing to me, and I think I know better than they do, so I don't listen to it." Your inability to take criticism may be so all-pervasive, however, that it devastates you no matter who is doing the criticizing, or what it is about.

Psychologist Lynn Diamond gives this explanation for the inability to take criticism:

> Nobody wants to fail. It's rejection. The fear of failure, or the fear of being rejected, is very great in all of us. "This report is good but I'd like you to change *x, y,* and *z*" or even "This report is unacceptable." It's the way the *buts* are given. So often we take them to mean not what we've done, but "you're not a good writer" or "you're not a good—." It has nothing to do with you and your project. You are not your product. You could be totally acceptable, but I may not like your writing. The whole goal of acceptance is to set a standard for your performance. "This report was good and I'd like you to change *x*" doesn't mean that you failed. It means you can do things to get better.

The following conditions make it easier to take criticism; try to achieve them in your work and personal situations:

A person knows your work
They already respect your abilities
They like you
They are trying to help you to improve (yourself or your product)

You have to learn to distinguish whether you are dealing with a knowledge-able, and critical, person who is providing beneficial advice, or with a sadistic and "always right" person who can never be pleased. In *For Each Other,* psychologist Lonnie Barbach describes the "put down" individual:

> People who feel insecure and inadequate often get into the right/wrong battle. They try to raise their self-image by being "right." One way of proving oneself right is to make the other person wrong. However, being right or wrong generally has very little to do with working out a good relationship. As a matter of fact, having to be right creates serious problems. Making someone feel wrong has an alienating effect.

If you are unable to take criticism, and you seek out only those who approve and praise you, in the long run you may waste time since you, and your work, may not improve. The runaway bestseller, *One Minute Manager,* expressed this idea quite simply: the key to success is one minute praisings *and* one minute reprimands.

Solutions: Usually the person who is unable to take criticism is also uncomfortable being critical. (That's the kind of person who says you look great even when you look terrible.) To work on your inability to take criticism, learn how to give it.

If you feel secure, you will be able to discriminate about the criticism that is offered, neither blindly accepting nor blindly rejecting it.

Look at criticism as observations, rather than judgments, and be objective about it. Is the criticism valid? If it is valid, how will you go about improving whatever has been criticized—the report, your appearance, the time you spend on the phone, how you handle meetings? If it is invalid, how can you explain to your criticizer that his comment is unwarranted?

Diamond suggests these techniques for getting over the inability to take criticism: (1) Make a list of all the things you do well to get away from the negatives; (2) Daydream. "Think of all the terrible things that could happen," Diamond says. "If you can [face] rejection, you can begin to deal with it. It's so easy to rationalize and blame the other person."

Set high (but realistic) standards and evaluate yourself and your work first, lessening the likelihood of criticism from authority figures or your loved ones. By prescreening your actions, words, products, and performance until you are satisfied, you will be more confidant that you can appraise the criticism objectively.

Rehearse what you might say to criticism, such as "Thank you, I'll consider that," "I see what you mean," "I disagree with you because . . . ," or "Let me get back to you on that." You can waste time if, because of your inability to take criticism, you bluntly accept all criticism, or you universally deny it has any value. Remember that some of the greatest achievers acknowledged the help that they received. It was their ability to take criticism, and apply it in a worthwhile way, that aided them in attaining their long-term goals. There's valuable criticism, and useless (and even wrong) criticism. Until you are able to take criticism, however, you will react to the fact that you are being criticized, rather than to the merits of the criticism.

Be open to criticism while you still stand firm in what you believe you should be doing; the payoff is more likely to come.

Commuting and Travel Time

Back and forth and back and forth and . . .

Each workday, America's 97 million workers commute to work, spending an average of 23 minutes each way. Most use a private vehicle—a notable 84 percent. For those who take public transportation (only 6.4 percent), travel time increases to 45 minutes each way. That works out to about four full workdays every month devoted just to commuting. Some may also have to take occasional or frequent long distance trips, by car, plane, or train, for business or pleasure. There's a lot of time at stake here, and people vary widely in their use of it. Some flip through magazines, some read others' newspapers, some snore, and some stare vacuously into space, daydreaming or planning their day's activities.

To creatively use your commuting or travel time, first, have a plan.

Don't commute or travel aimlessly day after day, trip after trip. Second, based on how you commute, and how long it takes, decide if you will use your commuting time to do your work, for recreational activities, or for some combination of the two.

If you commute alone by car there are safe, work-related tasks that you might consider doing. Donna Goldfein, a time management consultant who is founder and president of ESTE (Easy Steps Toward Efficiency), based in San Francisco, prefers to work while commuting by car. Before Goldfein drives to do an interview, or to see a client, she'll put her notes on a cassette tape, and play them back as she drives. Then, on the return trip, she'll listen to the taped interview, so she can transcribe it as soon as she returns to her office. Goldfein also has a "revolving tape program of motivational tapes" that she's acquired over the years. "I feel that puts me into a positive frame of mind, especially before I'm going to give a speech," says Goldfein, a former Miss Missouri who is also a consultant to airlines.

You can also use car commuting time for recreation and to reduce stress. Dr. Keith Sedlacek, co-author of *How to Avoid Stress Before It Kills You,* suggests, "When you're actually in the car there are a whole series of simple muscle relaxation techniques you can use. Even fifteen minutes is enough time to do that." Tapes may be purchased from centers such as Sedlacek's Stress Regulation Institute in New York. Another approach is to play stress reduction ("anti-frantic") music, such as "Spectrum Suite." That tape cassette is part of a series of tapes that provide soothing sounds that can be played while driving in the car (or, with earphones, while commuting by public transportation). For recreation, or education, there are numerous commercial and educational companies that sell prerecorded books that are ideal for commuters or travelers. If you have a busy life, however, you might find the silence while commuting alone a stress-reducer of another sort. "I like the quiet," says a woman who commutes two hours a day alone in her car. "It gives me time to think," she adds, explaining how the rest of her day she's around people and scurrying between activities.

Although a car pool minimizes worrying about safety, it can introduce interruptions by other passengers. One van pool commuter has learned how to deal with those situations in a way that might help others: if she wants to read, and someone else wants to talk, she answers whatever question or statement has been put to her, and immediately turns back to her reading, nipping a lengthy conversation before it starts.

Almost as many Americans walk to work as ride the trains, buses, and subways. Productive use of commuting time by foot is, of course, the utilization of that time for physical exercise, thinking, or errands. Dr. Merrill E. Douglass, president of the Time Management Center, a consulting firm in St. Louis, Missouri, has only a three-minute walk from his home to his office. The night before each workday, he prepares his "to do" list. The next morning, on his walk to the office, "I think about what I'm going to have to do when I get there," Douglass explains. (You may also review your "to do" list if you commute or travel by means of transportation other than walking.)

If you live within ten miles of your office, you might consider joining the two million Americans who currently bike to work. As William C. Wilkinson, III of the Bicycle Manufacturers Association of America, Inc., says: "Rather than being cooped up in a steel box of one type or another (car, bus, and so on), more and more of us are using our bikes to enjoy the fresh air and improve our fitness as a by-product of our work trip." (Once again, safety is your first commuting time concern, whether you travel by bike or car, or on foot.)

You might wish you could move your office closer to your home, or your home closer to your office. Or you might dream about becoming one of the 2.3 percent of American workers who work at home—especially when it's pouring rain or freezing cold outside. If, for the time being, commuting time is a reality for you, the more productively you make use of it, the less a source of wasted time and stress it will be.

Dr. Barbara Pletcher, executive director of the National Association for Professional Saleswomen, based in Sacramento, California, spends 150 days a year "on the road." Pletcher, a model of productivity and positive thinking, has practical suggestions for making the most of long-distance travel, whether it's once a week or once a year. Although long-distance travel may not seem to have the same direct productivity as staying in one place and, say, dictating twenty letters, it does allow you the time, and space, to look at long-range plans, often overlooked because of day-to-day short-term priorities. As Pletcher explains it:

> The reason I maintain my sanity when I travel is that I accept the fact that I am going to be gone as long as necessary. I don't fight it, or resent it, or get angry about it, the way many long-distance travelers do, saying, "Why am I here?" Instead, I say, "I'm going to be here, so I'm going to enjoy it." I use long-distance traveling to talk to people I would never talk to otherwise and to deviate from the certain rigidity of my schedule at home.
>
> When I'm on the road, and staying in a hotel, the phone isn't ringing constantly. Most of the time, no one even knows the number. Traveling gives me the time to think on another level. It's not decision-making or analyzing, it's just plain, what one of my friends calls, "garbage can thinking." "How will we get press next year?", not "I've got to get the newsletter to the printer this morning."

Here are other suggestions for making the most of long-distance travel, whether it's a two-hour train ride or an eight-hour plane trip:

- Sleep
- Socialize

- Read what you never seem to have the time for when you're at home (for example, a novel, old letters, some poetry)
- Daydream
- Meditate
- Reconsider your long-term goals and your plans to achieve them
- Take along stationery and catch up on your correspondence, or begin a personal journal
- Pick one time waster and map out a plan to overcome it

The Terrible Twos: Telephone and Television

More will be said about these two notorious time wasters later—the telephone in Chapter Four and the television in Chapter Six. For now, just start being aware of how much time you spend engaging in either activity, and what you should have—could have—been doing instead. Both are examples of habits which, uncontrolled, can eat up enormous amounts of time. Neither is in and of itself a bad habit; the frequency and duration of use determine its detrimental or beneficial effects. Start to note when you place calls; what you're doing when you receive calls (and if that effects how you deal with the caller); how long you usually stay on the phone and who is the first to say "I have to go now." Take stock of your television viewing as well, noting for starters if you watch specific programs or just have the TV on all the time.

Bad Habits

"That receipt has got to be around here somewhere."

Fortunately, with some effort, time-saving habits can replace time-wasting ones—from significant changes that require concerted and persistent effort in the way you now think, eat, and live, to elementary, easily learned tips. Whether the time-saving tips or techniques that you wish to use are major or minor, they will become habits only if they are consistently applied. You may not get extra dollars in your salary or straight *A*'s for these kinds of good habits, nor necessarily praise from your spouse, family, or friends, but your life will be more orderly and relaxed. You will find, to your amazement, that you suddenly have more time, and can do what you truly enjoy with less guilt and more of a sense of being "on top" of your work load.

If you procrastinate, or do too many things at once, you'll have to make an active effort to change if you want to manage your time more effectively. The only way to change is to make a conscious—and daily—effort in that direction. In *How People Change,* psychologist Alan Wheelis points out: "Personality change follows change in behavior. Since we are what we do, if we want to change what we are we must begin by changing what we do, must undertake a new mode of action." Don't expect to be pleased initially by those new habits, however better they may be. Wheelis notes: "The new mode will be experienced as difficult, unpleasant, forced, unnatural, anxiety-provoking. It may be undertaken lightly but can be sustained only by considerable effort of will. Change will occur only if such action is maintained over a long period of time."

Changing—and coping successfully with new situations—necessitates being in touch with who you are, and what you want. To embrace change means to be secure and self-determined. If you are thrown by change—new and unforeseen circumstances—you may also be reluctant to give up changing yourself and your bad habits, however ineffective they are.

In *What Life Should Mean to You,* psychologist Alfred Adler writes about change: "If we see emotions that apparently cause difficulties and run counter to the individual's own welfare, it is completely useless to begin by trying to change these emotions. They are the right expression of the individual's style of life, and they can be uprooted only if he changes his style of life." Change how you manage and spend your time, and you change your lifestyle.

Solutions: Decide what you want to change about yourself. (Don't blindly accept others' definitions for you; your procrastination may be a bad habit, or it may be purposeful and time effective.) If you put your effort into changing something that is wasting your time, you will at least begin with motivation from within (which may help you to keep going when you become impatient or discouraged).

Once you decide on a bad habit that you want to tackle—e.g., doing too many things at once, an inability to accept criticism, eating junk food, worrying, lack of exercise, interrupting while someone else is speaking—spend at least twenty-one days changing that habit. (As Young and Jones point out in *Sidetracked Home Executives,* the twenty-one days suggestion is based on research conducted by plastic surgeon Maxwell Maltz, author of *Psychocybernetics.* Maltz discovered that it took patients who had had a limb amputated twenty-one days to lose a ghost-image of their missing limb.)

Other solutions for changing bad habits—and there are whole books you can read on just this topic—include:

(1) Behavior modification techniques
(2) Hypnosis
(3) Biofeedback techniques
(4) Joining a self-help group
(5) Psychotherapy
(6) Increasing the discomfort that you feel because of a bad habit so you increase your motivation to change it

(7) Facing the fact that initially even changes for your own betterment may make you irritable, disagreeable, cranky, and less efficient
(8) Replacing the old, undesirable habit, such as unnecessary telephone interruptions, with a new, desirable habit, such as setting aside an hour or two for placing, and receiving, calls
(9) Applying the ABC Approach recommended in this book: (A) Know what you've got (which bad habit you want to change and what resources are available to you to successfully change); (B) Know what you want (what do you want to do, or have, instead); and (C) Using (A) and (B) to get what you want.

This chapter has shown how many personal issues—fear of success, fear of failure, an inability to take criticism, complaining, and so on—must be dealt with in order to effectively manage your time. Successfully dealing with those issues will enable you to achieve as much success as you would like. Does effective and creative time management spell success? Yes, the two go together.

One habit that is a common time waster, perhaps the most serious one of all, is disorganization, the subject of the next chapter. You may find that the practical suggestions for solving disorganization will help you to extend that comprehensive approach to other time wasters in your life.

TERMS

procrastination   perfectionism   low frustration tolerance

REFERENCES

ADLER, ALFRED. *What Life Should Mean To You.* New York: G.P. Putnam's Sons, 1931, 1958. Psychologist Adler deals with a whole host of vital areas, including occupation, love and marriage, and feelings of inferiority and superiority.

BARBACH, LONNIE. *For Each Other.* Garden City, N.Y.: Anchor Press/Doubleday, 1982.

BLANCHARD, KENNETH, and SPENCER JOHNSON. *The One Minute Manager.* New York: William Morrow and Company, Inc., 1982.

DOWLING, COLETTE. *The Cinderella Complex.* New York: Pocket Books, 1981.

DRUCKER, PETER F. *The Practice of Management: A Study of the Most Important Function in American Society.* New York: Harper & Row, Publishers, 1954. Drucker explores the necessary characteristics of a manager using illustrative examples from major U.S. companies.

ELLIS, ALBERT, and WILLIAM J. KNAUS. *Overcoming Procrastination.* New York: New American Library, 1979. Through case histories and examples,

this book stresses a nuts-and-bolts approach to overcoming procrastination and increasing your personal growth, that is part of the
school of RET (Rational-Emotive Therapy).

FRANKL, VIKTOR E. *Man's Search for Meaning.* New York: Pocket Books, 1939,
1963.

JACOBS, MARCIA. *The Excuse Book.* Los Angeles, Calif.: Price/Stern/Sloan, 1979.
A humorous book on excuses ranging from the believable to the
outrageous.

KUSHNER, HAROLD S. *When Bad Things Happen to Good People.* New York: Avon
Books, 1981.

LANG, DOE. *The Secret of Charisma.* New York: Wideview Books, 1980.

LEBOEUF, MICHAEL. *Working Smart.* New York: Warner Books, 1979. Discusses
everything from getting organized and dealing with interruptions to
melting the paper blizzard and keeping communications open.

MACKENZIE, R. ALEC, and KAY CRONKITE WALDO. *About Time! A Woman's Guide to
Time Management.* New York: McGraw-Hill Book Company, 1981.
Covers time-saving/time-wasting techniques and problems, geared to
the working mother with increased home and family time demands.

SCOTT, DRU. *How to Put More Time In Your Life.* New York: New American
Library, 1980. A thorough, five-step plan for time management dealing
with everything from prioritizing to procrastination.

STEFFEN, R. JAMES, editor. *The Ultimate Time Organizer.* Westport, Conn.:
Steffen, Steffen & Associates, Inc. A newsletter, issued every three
months, that covers work and personal time management, with
cartoons, highlights of related research, and problems and suggestions
from readers.

TEC, LEON. *Fear of Success.* New York: New American Library, 1978.

WHEELIS, ALLEN. *How People Change.* New York: Harper & Row, Publishers,
1973. Includes a telling story of how Wheelis himself never learned to
be completely comfortable "at play."

WAHLROOS, SVEN. *Excuses: How to Spot Them, Deal With Them, and Stop Using Them.*
New York: Macmillan Publishing Co., Inc., 1981. A look at the whys
and wherefores of excuses for practically every situation and age group.

YOUNG, PAM, and PEGGY JONES. *Sidetracked Home Executives.* New York: Warner
Books, 1981.

EXERCISES

1. Think of something that went wrong today, whether in your personal
life, at school, or on your job. Write down a short summary of the situation

and put it away. Make an effort not to tell anyone else about it. Tomorrow or the next day, look over the problem that you didn't burden anyone else with, and commend yourself for being able to compartmentalize your feelings and experiences (not making George suffer at home for what Joan did to you at the office, or vice versa).

2. The next time you have an idea, think of three reasons why it can't work. Make a list of those reasons, date it, put it aside, and then make your idea work anyway.

3. What do you think is your biggest time waster? Write it down.

How are you going to reduce, or eliminate, that time waster in your life?

4. Start keeping track of all the times you say "yes" when you should have said "no."

3
Becoming Organized and More Effective

*Organization is not an end in itself but a means
to the end. . . .*

PETER F. DRUCKER
(*The Practice of Management*)

GETTING ORGANIZED

There are those who appear to be "born" organizers, and those who seem to be forever misplacing and forgetting things. I must confess that I have always enjoyed creating order. When I was ten years old, and my mother became a full-time teacher, I looked forward to Tuesdays and Thursdays, the days I had been assigned to cleaning the house. Even "born" organizers are fallible, however. Ten years ago, for example, before I left for a two-month stay in Europe, I stored my watch and a few other pieces of jewelry in the basement of trusted relatives. Three months after my return, I went to retrieve my jewels, but was unable to find them, having failed to record just where I had put them. To this day, the jewelry has not been found. I realized I had "inherited" a trait from my grandmother—famous for saying "Hide it before you lose it"—who often hid things so well she never found them again.

The economic costs of disorder are dramatically driven home if you cannot find your valuables. Not as obvious, but costly nonetheless, are the wasted minutes each day—adding up to hours each month—reluctantly spent on treasure hunts, routinely searching for needed materials. Have you ever been locked out because you forgot your keys, or searched for an hour for your eyeglasses, hidden under yesterday's newspaper? Did you forget Harold's birthday? How about the meeting you missed because you mislayed the notice? How about those last-minute dashes to the liquor or grocery store just before guests arrived? Have you ever had to say, "I would have called sooner but I misplaced the slip of paper with your phone number on it"?

Organizing your possessions makes possible more effective use of your time at work, home, or school. Your goal is not to *look* organized, but to *be* organized. We have all heard of that rare individual who, faced with an elbow-high stack of papers, can miraculously pull out of it the one scrap of paper that he needs. To everyone but him, that stack is a mess; that mess, however, is *his* order.

If you are unlike that fictional character—and most of us are—becoming organized will take some effort. "Right places" for everything have to be created, so you'll know where to look for things later. Being organized means that you are able easily to locate one thing out of your many possessions. Your system should be able to handle information, envelopes, keys, stamps, the annual report, your summer beach shoes, last year's tax return, and your passport.

Being organized and more effective, however, also means that your activities are well-ordered, as well as your tangibles. Once again, your system should be a creative and flexible one. Becoming organized will free up hours of time that you may have been wasting. For example, do you now have even one hour during the day and at night that you use for concentrated work (e.g., planning, reading, thinking, reflecting over tomorrow's goals), or are you hurrying from task to task, allowing interruptions that you impose on yourself, or that others impose on you, to determine how you spend your time? The benefits of getting organized are quickly observed. Sam, 34, a disorganized professor, now is on top of things and able to handle more work and personal activities. Sam explains: "The more I manage to organize my time and work settings, the more I find I can get done." Sam accomplished this transformation by organizing his nonteaching work and leisure time into a fixed routine, "setting schedules and deadlines for projects."

In this chapter you will find a discussion of basic organizational principles, as well as several suggested systems; but one of your own creation is, if it works, perhaps even better. Follow this basic principle: Never make the *system* your focus; the system is supposed to make things *easier*. If you spend too much time creating, and maintaining, your "system," its purpose is lost.

Extreme disorder and extreme order will both prove to be wasteful of time.

You want to learn how to better organize your thoughts and actions as well as your possessions. Those three elements usually go together. There are exceptions, but often a cluttered desk reflects a cluttered mind. Throughout this chapter remember that your goal is becoming organized in *what* you do and *how* you do it. Apply an organizing principle to your activities, whether that system is chronological, thematic, general to specific, or specific to general. Impose an order on your work, or possessions, if they lack a "natural" order. Example: you have a conference to plan and you need an organizing principle for how you go about planning it. Create a principle by deciding tasks to do in the order of their importance, or in chronological order (e.g., contacting possible speakers, finding a place to have the conference, sending out brochures to possible participants).

Here are four simple organizational guidelines:

1. Eliminate clutter.
2. Everything in its place.
3. Plan what you have to do and make sure you do it.
4. Group and do similar tasks together.

Identifying Your Time Management Strengths

To aid you in getting organized, take a few moments to reflect on the time management strengths observed in the offices of effective and organized professionals:

1. Promptness.
2. Scheduling appointments based on accurate estimates of how long tasks (procedures) will take.
3. Notes and reminders written down in one book, not on little scraps of paper that create unmanageable piles.
4. Notes, and appointments, written in pencil to facilitate corrections.
5. Minimal personal phone or in-person interruptions. If such interruptions do occur, they are handled quickly (and in private).
6. Showing interest in work-related relations by: a) listening; b) making interesting small talk; c) keeping personal problems to oneself; and d) giving explanations in clear but not condescending language.
7. Maintaining a daily "things to do" list.
8. Deciding on, and following through on, short-term priorities and long-term plans.
9. Dealing with co-workers, clients, and employees in a formal but pleasant manner.
10. Scheduling personal time off or vacations.
11. Replacing files and tools in their proper place after each use.

How do you organize your business or personal affairs? Do you feel "in control" of your everyday activities, or as if you are bouncing off this crisis or that demand? What are your time management strengths? Does your present work or home routine take full advantage of those strengths? Perhaps you work best in long stretches, but you currently interrupt yourself for a one-hour lunch at the same time each day since that's what's expected of you, or so you think. Could you go to lunch, or order lunch in, so your work goals are aided?

In order to identify your time management strengths you have to consider what you are trying to accomplish, how long it should take you, and the best means to achieving the desired results. You may think that conducting business by phone saves time since you need not travel. If you are failing to establish personal and professional relationships, generally aided by in-person contact, the time saved on the phone may be costing you even more time in the long run.

You may find that you need to try, revise, and disregard certain schedules and procedures in order to become more organized and effective in what you do. As noted in the first chapter, as the demands on your time have changed—and as your goals and values have altered—you need to ask yourself whether your time budget reflects those changes.

Help yourself to identify your time management strengths by rating yourself in the key areas that follow. Note where you currently are, and where you need improvement. If three years ago your files were in order but you have failed to maintain an effective filing system, you have allowed your past organizational strength to become a current weakness—and your ratings below should reflect that change.

Time Management Consideration

	Poor	Good	Excellent
Address and phone number system	____	____	____
Things to do list	____	____	____
Telephone manner	____	____	____
Promptness	____	____	____
Filing system	____	____	____
Resource materials library	____	____	____
Short-term planning	____	____	____
Long-term planning	____	____	____
Daily scheduling	____	____	____
Effectiveness of meetings	____	____	____
Delegating	____	____	____
Additional training	____	____	____

Remember that you are trying to find a system of organizing your activities and possessions (or tools) that is best for you. We all have thousands of activities or actions we must follow up on—from Aunt Rose's birthday to filing an annual tax return. The ramifications may be as dire on a personal level as on a business level. What is at issue is: What organizational system will best utilize your time management strengths?

Sharpening Decision-Making Skills

Becoming more organized and effective means sharpening your decision-making skills. In order to do that, develop well-conceived rules upon which you make decisions. In that way, you will avoid the need to ponder every little situation. Ask yourself these questions any time a decision has to be made:

> How important is this to do?
> What are the consequences of doing it? of not doing it?
> What are the consequences of doing it now? doing it later?
> How does this new idea (situation, request, etc.) fit in with what's important to me today? for the rest of my life?

By applying the rule of "How can I best use my time *now*" you will sharpen your decision-making skills. You will also sharpen your decision-making skills, and save time, if you focus on learning, not assessing blame. If a new idea or approach is suggested to you, ask yourself: Is it faster (or better)? Is it slower (or less effective)? What makes the difference? Reducing or eliminating the time wasters discussed in the last chapter, as well as becoming more organized, will facilitate your decision-making skills.

Distinguishing Daily Priorities from Busywork

If at the end of the day you cannot point to one or more activities that were productive, you have a problem. You are allowing busywork, whether related to work or personal affairs, to interfere with accomplishing your short-term priorities "one day at a time" and your long-term goals. Most office jobs in which someone else assigns work to you minimize this problem by having a superior do the prioritizing for you. However, you may be failing to accomplish job-related goals for your own advancement. For example, if you need to rewrite your resumé, the burden will be on you to find the time to do it during your non-work hours.

Busywork is another term for low priority tasks. Reading a trade journal may, or may not, be a priority task. Having a second cup of coffee as you read the second or third city newspaper is probably busywork, unless you work for a newspaper clipping service. You may be spending much of your time wishing you "did more" after work, but because of poor planning or procrastination you are still watching TV or on the phone more than you want to be.

Two of the biggest inhibitors to being organized and effective are paperwork and telephone calls. Paperwork can generate hours of busywork. A distinction has to be made between high priority paperwork, discussed in the next chapter under "Correspondence," and doing the paper *shuffle,* whereby papers (junk mail, low priority pieces of paper, material to be filed or discarded) are moved around, fondled but unread, or piled up (and glanced at without any definite action being taken) in a disorganized fashion, consuming time and space. You've probably already heard lots of advice on paperwork, like "Handle a piece of paper only once" or "Dot a piece of paper each time you handle it until it has the measles and you do something with it." Doing the paper shuffle, described more extensively in the next chapter, can be an enormous time waster. Minimize your chances of falling into the paper busywork trap by eliminating distracting papers as much as possible. File it. Answer it. Throw it out. Put it with other papers of a similar nature and take care of them all at once.

Telephone interruptions may also consume hours of valuable time. If you take each and every call as it comes in, how do you expect to be organized—at the office or at home? Try scheduling a telephone hour for placing calls—you have more control over when you place calls than when they come in—and budget that hour into your daily schedule. You might also try instituting a period during the morning and the afternoon at the office when you prefer to receive incoming calls. Write lists, for yourself or your secretary, if you have one, of telephone interruptions that are permissible at times other than your designated "telephone incoming call hours." (The more strictly you adhere to your "no calls now" policy, the more valuable this way of organizing your day will become.) At home, consider that, except for emergencies, telephone calls should not be allowed to interfere with your dinnertime (often the only time some families have to interact with each other). Say to callers: "We're having dinner now. Can I call you back later?" If you're consistent, your friends, relatives, and even business associates will learn to respect your personal time budget.

ORGANIZING TOOLS AND TECHNIQUES

"Do" Lists

Mental order is even more important than cataloging your possessions. One of the most effective tools in time management is knowing what you want to do. Maintain a "things to do" list, and write it down. Make sure it's readily accessible to you.

There are several approaches to creating a "things to do" list. Such a list makes it more likely that you will act on important matters. Merrill E. Douglass, director of the Time Management Center in Missouri, gives this advice about effective "to do" lists:

> Daily planning—which for most people will take the form of a things-to-do list—is the step after a weekly plan is completed. Establish your objectives for the day. Write out all the planned activities for accomplishing the day's objectives. Rate them according to priority, and estimate the amount of time required for each one.
>
> Frankly, the To-Do lists that are kept by most people provide only marginal benefits. The reason is that most To-Do lists are a random collection of activities which have very little, if anything, to do with the purpose for which people work. Furthermore, most people have such a poor grasp of their objectives and priorities that a To-Do list can hardly be an improvement. Thirdly, almost no one gives real thought to how long things take. As a consequence, most To-Do lists contain far more than could be done in any given day. An excellent To-Do list asks a very critical question: "How long is it going to take me to do it?"

Here are some alternative ways for creating effective "to do" lists for your work and personal goals:

(A) Divide your list to reflect how you arrange your day, such as:

Before Work (or School)
During Work (or School)
After Work (or School)

Within each section, fill in the appropriate activities.

(B) Follow a simpler chronological system, listing the key activities you want to accomplish that day, starting with number one. As you finish an activity, check or cross it off, and go on to the next thing you have to do. A sample of this approach follows:

1. Call airline to confirm tickets.
2. Write memo for meeting.
3. Duplicate memo for distribution.

(C) Write items down in order of descending importance, putting the major daily goal as number one (and not going on to number two until number one is done). Obviously, you will have to break down large tasks—writing a term paper, decorating the living room—into smaller steps, or you may take weeks to get to number two. Here's a sample of that approach:

1. Write memo for meeting.

2. Duplicate memo for distribution.
3. Call airline to confirm tickets.

(D) Use the verb-noun principle discussed and developed in Chapter One. That system is especially useful if you have to complete a major project but you find yourself procrastinating or getting distracted by activities of lesser importance.

Fill in the blank "things to do" list that follows (or use one of your own design), and check off each item as you complete it. Include all personal and professional tasks. Decide which organizing principle you will follow, and start by attacking whatever "to do" item is first on your list.

Things to Do Today

Date _____

		Done
1.	_____	_____
2.	_____	_____
3.	_____	_____
4.	_____	_____
5.	_____	_____
6.	_____	_____
7.	_____	_____
8.	_____	_____
9.	_____	_____
10.	_____	_____

The idea is not to become a list maker, spending more time in creating lists than in completing your priority tasks. List making is merely a way to organize your obligations—and a way to learn to do thoroughly one thing at a time.

Practically everyone I interviewed who finds list making useful preferred writing a "to do" list for the following day right before going to bed; some said it actually helped them to sleep better. John, 31, a self-employed glass designer, says: "Between midnight and one, I make a list of items to do the next day. Some are important to do that day and I do those first. Others may be done another day, but I write them down when I think of them."

Creating a Personal Planning Calendar

Bonnie, 28, vice-president of a bank, would be as disorganized as the rest of us if not for her personal planning calendar. Without fail, she records all work and personal commitments on that calendar. "It helps me to sleep at night," Bonnie explains. In one place she has birthdays to remember, upcoming meetings, seminars she will have to attend, vacation days, and so forth. Your planning calendar can be a wall calendar, or a daily appointment book, but the consensus is that it should be one or the other but not both. Depending on the work or personal demands on your schedule, you might need to have a calendar of the entire year at your fingertips if, let's say, you want to see when in April you're scheduled to speak in Denver and when in June you're scheduled to do a seminar in St. Paul. Try to get into the habit of not just recording "events" but also preparation time. For instance, you have to give a talk on Saturday, May twenty-first, and, of course, that is noted in your daily appointment book and on your wall chart. Have you also noted what hours or days you will be devoting to the preparation of that talk, including research time and practice sessions?

Remember: apply the same rules of organization to your activities as you will apply to organizing your possessions. Eliminate clutter (unnecessary time wasters and interruptions) and poor planning (disorder).

Avoid cluttering your personal planning calendar with irrelevant information and, if possible, use pencil so corrections are facilitated. Your planning calendar should provide you with an overview of specific commitments for the days, weeks, and months ahead. Make sure you note personal plans or you might forget to follow up on them. Consider entering "free day" on your planning calendar, or you may never find the time for one.

The importance of a personal planning calendar is emphasized when, because of failure to maintain one, appointments are missed, deadlines ignored, or details of upcoming events are confused. Just in the past week, for example, Gloria showed up a week early for a party, Jim and Lila forgot their daughter's wedding anniversary, Dorothy completely forgot to attend her friends' concert recital, as promised, and George had to cancel two meetings because he had failed to note that he would be away on jury duty during those times. Alas, creating a personal planning calendar will not prevent others, who lack one, from disappointing you. However, it ensures that you will be more organized and efficient.

A variation on the personal planning calendar is the personal notebook. Like the calendar, all notes, incoming and outgoing phone calls, new addresses and phone numbers, ideas, and random thoughts are jotted down in one place as they occur. The notebook, such as a small spiral, looseleaf, or bound notebook, if possible, is carried with you at all times—in your pants or jacket pocket, pocketbook or attaché case. The advantage of using one notebook, what travel writer Theodore Fischer calls his "Everything Notebook," is that you avoid the disorganized mess of lots of little slips of papers that may be lost, misplaced, or in need of being transferred to another source. (You may still decide to transfer some of your notes and memos, but you always have your master chronological source to refer to.) The Everything Notebook is labeled with the current year. If more than one notebook is used during the year, each volume is numbered consecutively. As Fischer explains:

> This way I have only one source to go to; only one thing to grab when the phone rings. Every bit of business goes into the notebook. Each one lasts about two to three months. I'd feel undressed if I didn't have this book with me. One other thing about the notebooks: each time one is full, I have to decide which names, numbers, and addresses to copy into the new book. This provides a valuable opportunity for taking personal, social, and professional stock because you have to determine which names are still important, which are no longer important, which may be potentially important. It's like a mortal's version of the Book of Life.

File Systems

The main types of materials that will fill your home or office files are:

1. Originals of incoming correspondence and/or interoffice memos
2. Copies of outgoing corespondence
3. Important papers or records for permanent safekeeping (e.g., contracts, company policy statements, employee evaluations, receipts or records for taxes, and birth and marriage certificates)
4. Reference or research materials
5. Warranties and instruction booklets
6. Announcements about upcoming events (trips, cultural or educational activities, invitations, meetings)

How many files you need will depend upon the kind of job you do, and how much information or material you want or need to have available. (The term *file* as it is used throughout this section refers to the conventional beige manila letter-size file folder. *File* could also mean oversized envelopes, floppy disks, or magnetic diskettes, or index cards.)

Keep active and inactive items separated, so that you can find day-to-day and priority materials quickly.

Once you decide which files you need ready access to, the major battle against disorganization of papers and research materials is won. Once you create a system, based upon inactive and active categories, it will be much easier to find things.

Within your active files, you can sort papers by importance (the priority approach), according to immediacy of response required, by category, by author, or by date.

You can arrange research material alphabetically or by subjects (broad or narrow). You can put important documents in a file broadly labeled "important records" or put each record or document in a separate file; those files can then be organized by category or alphabetically or chronologically.

There is one type of written job or school-related material that must be filed, and it might be helpful to keep that file separate from the day-to-day originals and copies of memos that you also need to file. These crucial documents are the CYA ("Cover Your Ass," in the Army's always colorful lingo) materials. If a problem arises a day, a week, or a year from now, you can show, through your carefully filed records (the CYA file), that you were not at fault, because you had touched second base, notified the appropriate governmental agency within the filing deadline, or made the necessary payment.

Try devising a new or improved filing system:

Step 1: Divide a blank sheet of paper into two columns labeled "Active" and "Inactive."

Step 2: Make a list of all the types of materials that you need to file, such as incoming correspondence, cancelled checks, and documents, placing each category under the "Active" or "Inactive" heading (duplicating entries under both headings, if appropriate).

Step 3: Select one type of material to be filed—e.g., incoming correspondence—and decide what filing system you will use.

Step 4: On a blank sheet of paper, work out on paper how you plan to file that one category, noting the organizing principle that you will follow, the system to be used, who will have ready access to these files, and a way in which active material can be rendered inactive.

Step 5: On separate sheets, repeat this paper planning process for your remaining categories.

Step 6: In order of importance, begin to implement your filing systems, purchasing any necessary supplies. Continue until your files are created.

Step 7: Maintain your planning notes since they will help you if at any point you forget any of the details behind your system.

Another filing system that some effective managers find useful is called a "tickler file." The system works like this: A file folder is made for each day of the month so that there are thirty or thirty-one file folders numbered 1 through 31. There are also twelve files, one for each month. Any follow-up items are placed in the appropriate "to do" month file; as the month becomes current, pieces of paper are moved to the specific date (file) on which the action is to be carried out. The tickler file requires some time to set up. For it to be effective, you have to maintain, and use it, as consistently as your daily planning calendar. For example, you might buy enough birthday and anniversary cards for the entire year. Address the envelopes and place the blank cards in the appropriate month when you will need one. When the month arrives, you move the card to the file for the date on which you should inscribe and mail that card. If you have season tickets to sports events, concerts, and so forth, you could file the appropriate tickets with the correct month, moving the tickets to the appropriate date as that month becomes current. If you use a computer or word processor, there is software available that has calendars and reminders that perform a function that is similar to the "tickler" file. (You still, however, need some kind of filing system for placing the actual correspondence, memos, cards, or tickets that you are following up on.) Computerized reminder systems, however, still necessitate "booting up" your computer and looking at the calendar in question, just as tickler files must be actively referred to if they are to be effective organizational tools.

Types of possible filing systems include: filing cabinets; document folders; magnetic diskettes (for use with computers/word processors); envelopes; boxes (cardboard, metal, or plastic); containers (decorative or plain); notebooks; garbage can; or bulletin board. By using any of these systems, you free up your memory for more important storage—the kind that can't be handled by filing.

Organizing Desks and Bookcases

Inside Your Desk

It's far easier to organize the paper clips in your drawer than it is to get some order from masses of unrelated pieces of paper. There are dozens of effective and inexpensive drawer organizers that you can purchase.

Stamps	Eraser	Paper clips	Push pins
Miscellaneous		Rubber bands	
Pens and pencils			

Your primary goal is to avoid unmanageable and disorderly piles of unrelated supplies and materials in your desk. You want everything readily accessible, and in a place of its own. Keep extras of all your supplies, in ample quantity, in a supply closet or some other storage area.

On Top Of Your Desk

Organizing the top of your desk is quite an individual matter. If you have a problem concentrating at your desk, try experimenting with adding or removing items—e.g.. family portraits, pencil holders, paper weights, or calendars—to see if your work habits improve. You should avoid keeping anything other than what you are currently working on on top of your desk—too many files or projects can provoke the "doing too much at once" syndrome. Jessica, 60, a middle management executive, has such a cluttered desk (and office) that she has to find a vacant office at her company to meet with clients. "I never get around to cleaning my desk because I always feel I should be doing *real* work," Jessica explains. Keeping your desk organized so, at the very least, you need not apologize to visitors *is* part of your job. Fortunately, once the initial organizational system is implemented, it takes just minutes each day to maintain it. Your desk is just part of an area that should be organized for work efficiency. (See drawing on page 62.)

Books, Magazines, and Other Reading Materials

Books, magazines, newspapers, journals, pamphlets, and other reading materials pile up quickly, and can become a major obstacle to an organized office or home. One couple has let the problem get so out of hand that whenever they move, their multiple cartons of unsorted reading materials move with them. The thought of going through those boxes, organizing useful materials and discarding the rest, is more awesome than spending the time and money to continually transport those weighty boxes.

Before it gets out of hand, you will find it a great time saver to evolve an orderly system for the accumulation, and disposal, of reading materials. Have a clear notion of whether you will sort or discard on a daily, weekly, monthly, or yearly basis. (Otherwise, you may find yourself just indiscriminately throwing out piles of unread materials when the volume is just too much to bear.) Making a list of all incoming publications will be useful for organizing your storage and retrieval systems.

There are a variety of temporary storage systems for reading materials—baskets for the floor or your desk, lucite holders, vertical cardboard units, elaborate 48- or 96-compartment literature organizers, etc.—that you can use for sorting and storing reading materials before you examine them. (You might also consider the altruistic and tax benefits of donating reading materials, that you might otherwise throw out, to college or local libraries, prisons, shelters, or schools.

Bookcases should fit the space available to you and be of the correct size for what you have to shelve. If you are reluctant to take the time to measure the height needed for each shelf, get adjustable shelves.

Arranging books by category, author, or some other system geared to

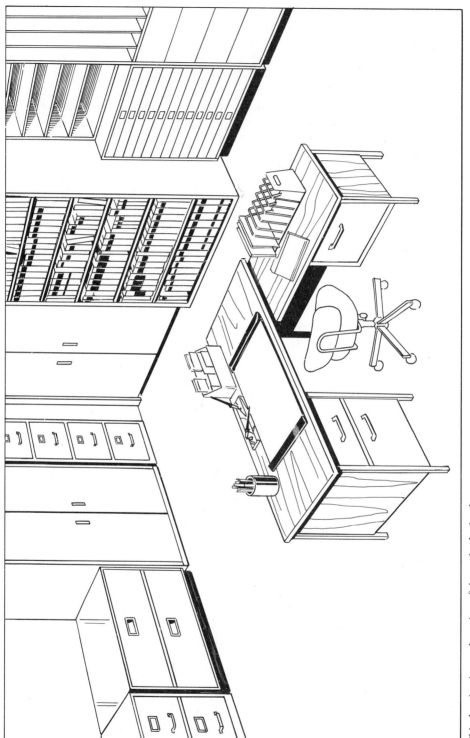

This drawing is an adaptation of the author's sketch.

your needs will, in the long run, save you time, but initially you will have to devote hours to completing that task. Organizing expert Stephanie Winston suggests rearranging one section of your bookshelves at a time, using empty cardboard boxes to store the books as you reorder one part of your bookcase. In *Getting Organized,* Winston writes: "To start, count out thirty or forty books as the 'work portion,' or, if the shelves are already divided by panels, work within one panel. Begin with the highest or lowest shelf of the bookcase on the far left. With a clear starting point you can easily keep track of the ground you've covered."

Just as you made a list of incoming magazines and other reading materials, now make a list of the categories of books that you have. If you find that your collection is basically just one or two types of books—let's say reference books such as the dictionary, *Bartlett's Quotations,* and works of fiction—you might decide tnat it is more efficient for you to organize within the fiction section, by author or by title, with a second section for reference books, by title.

In the Home Office

If you work at home, you have more pressure to become, and stay, organized than most others since visitors to your home may also have access to your office. (It's pretty hard to close your "office" off to all other family members or guests if it serves as a den or playroom at night.) Even if your home office is a completely separate room, the more organized you are, the less likely that anyone wandering through it—including children—can misplace or damage your files, manuscripts, drawings, books, or whatever. Everything you've learned about being organized—and everything you'll learn about time management at work in ·he chapter that follows—applies to a home office, whether a separate room or the corner of your bedroom.

You might consider purchasing a complete "office" in a cabinet, sold by numerous furniture companies to solve the space and organizational problems of those who must work in multifunctional areas. These cabinets open to reveal clearly defined sections for such office needs as files, reference materials, supplies, a typewriter or adding machine, even an office phone. When closed, the unit is a big box. Aesthetically and financially, these organizational solutions may not appeal to you. However, the concept is worth noting: everything in its place, and close to the point of use.

Obviously your organizational problems will be somewhat different if your home office is a separate room in a spacious home, or the corner of the living room in a two-bedroom apartment that houses a family of four. Certain considerations are universal, however: what are the essential supplies, and pieces of equipment, that have to be nearby and what can be stored elsewhere—in closets, other rooms, even other locations? Brenda, 39, a children's book editor and author and the mother of a two-year-old, works out of her two-bedroom apartment. This is Brenda's advice for someone working out of a home office: "You have to set up a separate time and a separate space to work. You have to create space and time whether it is in the kitchen, bedroom, or inside the bathtub. That's your space and you go to it. You have to have your own files and desk. If you don't have space for it, use part of the closet. Even my daughter, who's two, knows that she is never to touch the files on top of my desk. She'll get a pencil off the desk, but she won't touch those piles."

With the increased computerization of certain types of office work, more and more workers may be working at home. There are physical and social problems inherent in the home office situation that you should consider. See the section on Structuring Time in the last chapter of this book for further suggestions about organizing your time in a home office environment.

Disorganization frustrates the best attempts to effectively use your time. There are some who gain enormous pleasure from cleaning out their closets and ordering their activities or possessions. There are others who have an emotional attachment to things or who lack an affinity in this regard. Continue reading this book; you may find the motivation, and answers, to help you with this dilemma. However, it's a lot easier to find a professional to organize your possessions than it is to find someone to organize your activities and work commitments. You are the only one who can organize your work or leisure activities. In the next two chapters, you will learn additional solutions to becoming more organized at the office and at home. In the last chapter, the section on Structuring Time will provide specific suggestions on organizing your time according to whether you are a housewife, student, self-employed, or a nine-to-five worker. There are lots of ways to become organized and more effective in your work or leisure activities. One rule that helps in creating order is the following one:

Promise less, deliver more.

By following this rule, you come out ahead. Expectations are lower so you can come out a winner. If you promise too much, even if you deliver more, you may be judged as less effective. Allow yourself enough time—to get a job done, to get to an appointment on time, to reorganize and maintain your paperwork, files, and belongings. Consider organizing your week around your work and personal needs and commitments. Once you have a master plan—and you feel confident about it—others will respond to your priorities. If you answer the question, "What are you doing this holiday weekend?" with self-assurance, what you are actually doing is less important.

Whether your answer is "We're going to the beach" or "I'm staying home and reading a few books" matters mostly to you and those closest to you. If you are doing what you want to do, you are more effective. Being organized is a tool to increasing your effectiveness.

TERMS

tickler file   magnetic diskette

REFERENCES

DRUCKER, STEPHEN. "Home as Office: Mergers That Work," *New York Times,* March 31, 1983, pp. C1, C6.

HEWES, JEREMY JOAN. *Worksteads: Living and Working in the Same Place.* Garden City, N.Y.: Doubleday & Company, Inc., 1981. Based on interviews with one hundred persons who work at home, Hewes writes a glowing endorsement of this type of lifestyle.

MOSKOWITZ, ROBERT. *How to Organize Your Work and Your Life.* Garden City, N.Y.: Dolphin Book/Doubleday, 1981.

VOGEL, CAROL. "Getting Your Books Put in Apple-Pie Order," *New York Times,* February 12, 1981, pp. C1, C16. Tips on organizing your library, including a list of freelance librarians you can hire for this purpose.

WINSTON, STEPHANIE. *Getting Organized.* New York: Warner Books, 1978. Winston suggests three organizing principles ("Use a single notebook for notes to yourself," "Divide up a complex problem into manageable segments," and "After articulating a small group of projects, rank them by number according to how *aggravating* they are") and covers managing paper, storage basics, financial planning, and organizing specific rooms (kitchen, children's rooms, etc.).

EXERCISES

1. Select a place (the top of your desk, the front hall closet) or an activity (the monthly report, a term paper, a cocktail party) and apply the "who, what, why, when, where, and how" analysis to organize it.

2. What are the organizing principles for each of the major storage areas (closets) in your work place or home? If you lack satisfactory organizing principles, create them now.

3. Write down where you keep (or would like to keep) each item listed below.

Item	Current Location	Alternative Location
house keys	_____	_____
pens	_____	_____
sewing supplies	_____	_____
summer clothes	_____	_____
winter clothes	_____	_____
the dictionary	_____	_____
photo albums	_____	_____
sunglasses	_____	_____
batteries	_____	_____

4
Improving Your Time
at Work

*More men are killed by overwork than the
importance of the world justifies.*

RUDYARD KIPLING
(*The Phantom Rickshaw*)

In some ways, the structure of the traditional work environment aids time management: although there may be autonomy within each task, employers set rules or guidelines about when to arrive, when to leave, what days to take as holidays, and, often, what to wear. Procedures for evaluating performance and determining a raise are not always as clearly defined.

Within this framework, then, workers are to a large extent on their own. You may know that you have to go to a meeting on Wednesday, but no one tells you how to get the most out of it. So don't let the external structure of your job misguide you that if you just show up each day, follow the rules, and do what's asked, you'll be making the best use of your time (and guaranteeing success). The hard part of your workday is completely up to you. Although following company policy may seem commendable, that's the very least that's expected. Those rules go along with the job: observe them or quit. But what you do with the work that you're given is what will help you stand out from Sally or Fred, sending you up the ladder, or back to the mailroom.

When it comes to work (or school), ask yourself this question: Is my performance judged on the quality of what I do, the volume of work I generate or complete, or whether or not I meet deadlines? Perhaps it's all three or, perhaps, it changes from day to day, month to month, or project to project. This is a question that you should be continually asking.

Rule number one to improve your time at work is: Find out what is expected of you.

First do what's expected; the extras are the gravy. If you're hired to make the coffee, but you're wheeling and dealing instead, the person who hired you might not be as pleased as you thought she would be.

69

UNDERSTANDING YOUR WORK ENVIRONMENT

Cindy punches in each morning exactly at nine and goes to the three-walled, metal cubicle in a high rise office building where she will spend the next eight hours, minus one hour for lunch. On the surface she is an excellent, reliable worker. She does not need to take work home; she seems to accomplish it all within her workday. She takes two weeks off each year for her paid vacation, all the sick days and personal leave that she is allowed, and seems always to be busy. Underneath the "perfect employee" facade, however, are these realities:

- at least two hours a day are spent on the phone with personal calls.
- Cindy is not given enough to do so she reads mystery novels or magazines, carefully concealed from her boss, whose office is many cubicles away.
- She spends a lot of time in traveling to and from the bathroom, chatting all the way.

Those who work hard and are surprised by Cindy's lackadaisical attitude might believe that management soon "found out" Cindy's ways. They didn't! Cindy learned how to get management's expectations lowered to her own standard. When Cindy left to take a better offer (and more money), she was sent on her way with roses and glowing letters of recommendation. There are many who would not want to trade places with Cindy even if they could. Job satisfaction means accomplishing a job that you value, not just getting paid for sitting at a desk all day doing as little as you can get away with.

Some office workers say: "I can only get things done before everyone else gets here" (or after everyone else leaves). The result: they work seven to five or nine to seven, but not all that time is spent well. Their work-related time is longer, yet not necessarily more productive.

Take a hard, critical look at your workday. Work out on paper exactly what the time demands are on you.

Managing your time better at work may mean redesigning your work space so you have better working conditions. It might mean asking your boss if you can get a door for your cubicle, because socializing with employees has so gotten out of hand that you find you have less and less uninterrupted time. You might even consider talking to your employer about the possibility of flexible working hours, also known as flexitime—an alternative to traditional fixed work schedules that gives the employee freedom to choose times of arrival and departure. "It should be emphasized," observes Simcha Ronen, author of *Flexible Working Hours,* "that the choice given to the employee is restricted to variations in times present at work and the distribution of working hours, but does *not* apply to the total number of working hours required by the employment contract." So flexitime might help you bypass the two-hour traffic jam that you continually face when you have to be in by nine, but you'll still have to put in your thirty-five, forty, or whatever number of total hours.

It's up to you, as much as possible within managerial or economic restraints, to make your work environment as efficient, pleasant, and functional as possible. Apply the conceptual and practical organizing principles that you learned in the previous chapter: everything in its place, eliminate clutter, have readily available the tools and supplies you frequently need.

Becoming More Efficient

Correspondence and Paperwork

Practically all office jobs require writing, and answering, letters; even if you delegate the actual writing of your correspondence to a secretary or an assistant, an incoming letter has to be read and a decision made about whether it should be answered, and what form that answer will take.

Correspondence can become so time-consuming that the real work never gets done. It can also be so integral to your work that without it, there will *be* no real work. It's best to use correspondence as a warm-up for the more demanding, or creative, parts of your job. Michael Korda, editor-in-chief at Simon & Schuster publishing company as well as the best-selling author of *Power!* and *Success!,* finds that doing his own mail in the morning is a way he uses his "energy potential," as he puts it in *Success!* Writes Korda: ". . . then I decided that it was important to begin the day by accomplishing something, however trivial. I would spend the first hour of the morning answering mail. I would take no telephone calls, see nobody. I treated the mail as a separate, important but finite block of work. When I had read it, answered it, taken the necessary action where action was called for and gotten rid of it *all,* I had a cup of coffee, took a walk around the office to see what was happening, then went back to answer telephone calls on a priority basis. It was not very long before I began to look forward to my first hour—it gave me a sense of accomplishment and purpose." Korda essentially found a way to turn the tedious task of answering correspondence into an effective time management tool.

If you have a tendency to procrastinate about correspondence, address the envelopes for the letters you have to write and keep them in front of you. It may motivate you to write the letters that have to go inside those envelopes.

Dictating correspondence into a tape recorder is useful if you are experiencing "writer's block," or if you have a secretary to transcribe the tapes for you. If you lack a secretary, dictating letters may waste time since you will have to transcribe the tape and then edit your verbal comments into acceptable prose.

You can save time by having several "types" of letters for you, or your secretary, to adapt according to specific circumstances, such as business letters that say "Thank you," "Sorry, no jobs are currently available," "May I have the following information . . ." and so forth. These "samples" differ from a form letter in that they are adapted to a specific person and situation; they are not photocopied nor do they resemble a letter that has been done en masse on a word processor.

If you do use a word processor, and the body of the letter is the same with only the inside address and greeting different, minimize your chances of having that fact known by making your modified "form" letter as short as possible. One-to-two page single-spaced letters are often a "tip-off" that they have been done on a word processor.

Unless you decide to ignore incoming correspondence, or consider delay an asset, letters, like phone calls, should be responded to as promptly as possible.

To save time if you communicate with someone within your company, consider writing a brief interoffice memo, rather than a more time-consuming formal business letter.

Some time experts, such as Alan Lakein, advise: "Handle each piece of paper only once." That advice, like all time management advice, has to be tailored to your own needs. I used to follow that policy with a passion, handling paper only once, then either filing it, following up on it, or throwing it out. That policy, however, left too little time for my concentrated work. With more sensitivity to my own work needs, I learned to put all papers but the occasional "immediate attention" item into files labeled by the type of material—e.g., Upcoming Activities, Clippings to File, Correspondence to Answer, Information Requests. Except for urgent priority matters, which are handled immediately, I now work on an entire file so my efforts are maximized. I take control of my paperwork rather than letting it control me. (If you have a tendency to procrastinate, are unable to discriminate between priority and low-payoff correspondence, or if out of sight is out of mind, consider the more conventional time management approach of handling a piece of paper just once.)

As was noted in the previous chapter on becoming organized, the key is to set up a filing system that works for you. It doesn't matter if it's alphabetic, chronologic, thematic, or whatever. All that counts is that you can find things in a fast and reliable manner.

How you handle copies of materials can be crucial; over time, paper has a way of piling up and becoming unmanageable. A lawyer I know makes two copies of each memo or letter; one is filed by subject; the other is filed chronologically. This way he has two ways of relocating it at some point in the future. Do you regularly copy all important memos? Do you make notes about telephone conversations and put them into your files? Keeping track of what you accomplish each day is a way of gaining control of your time. Do not, however, make the written record, or copies of that record, as important as the work itself.

Mechanical Helpers

Whether it's a word processor, a memory typewriter, a computer, a calculator, or a photocopying machine, remember that mechanical helpers can be time-saving tools, but they can also be more trouble than they're worth. The catch is that you may not understand the usefulness of a certain type of machine until you've learned how to use it competently enough to put it into your everyday operations. If you want to experiment with a new type of machinery at your job, have a machine installed for a two-week tryout period. Build into your work schedule the learning time that you will need to gain mastery over it (including careful study of the user's manual). Initially, it may take more—not less—time to complete a task, but in the long run you may save time. When photocopying machines became common in office buildings, for example, the need to make copies increased—and not just copies of documents that would have been carboned previously. New ways to use the copier emerged. Until employees learned the proper use of photocopying, they, or their assistants, were spending more time duplicating than before (even though it was now faster and easier). A best-selling novelist's attitude about a word processor when asked if he planned to get one (he has written on the same manual typewriter from the beginning of his career): No, he was not going to get one, but he might get one for his secretary. So, if your system is working, don't introduce a new mechanical way of doing it just because it's available. It just might cost you time.

The Telephone

The telephone is a tool or a weapon, depending upon how you use it, or let it use you. Using the telephone for a long-distance phone interview may be the most important work-related task you accomplish on a given day; allowing numerous personal or business calls to interrupt you at crucial times when you are working may be frustrating, as well as time wasting. Some workers allow personal calls at their offices only during a certain hour of the day, and only for a certain length of time. Others make it clear that personal calls, whenever they are received, must be brief and to the point, related to a specific question such as, "When do you expect us over tonight?" rather than just a way of "shooting the breeze."

If you're having trouble figuring out just how your telephone time is spent, or wasted, consider keeping a phone log. Start logging all outgoing and incoming calls, noting the duration of each call. Try to discern patterns in your personal and business calls.

If you are prone to compulsive talking, set a time limit for your calls. Even if you're not, try to have a clear idea of what you want to say, and how long you will allow yourself to say it, whenever you initiate a call.

Secretaries, phone machines, and answering services can be helpful in the battle against the telephone, but only if used well. Most phone machines have monitors, so that you can screen calls and decide whether or not to pick up, without callers knowing you are there. Sometimes you may decide it is better to take a call since returning a call can take even more time.

Some people find it useful to have categories of callers, or types of calls; on this list, personal and business contacts are classified into one of the categories—Always Put Through, Never Put Through, Always Take Message and Say I'll Return the Call. This system can be quite effective, since it eliminates that awkward interaction when a secretary says, "I'll check to see if she's in," and although the caller knows that the secretary is querying her boss, the secretary soon returns, saying, "No, I'm afraid she's not in at the moment, but she will return your call."

If you want to use the phone rather than letting it use you, consider memorizing, and using, this useful little phrase: "I can't talk right now." If you want, add "Can I get back to you?" (You may also wish to advise your friends of any work-related policies, such as "No personal calls at the office, unless it's an emergency.") Here are some other phrases to try if you have trouble getting off the phone, or telling the caller that you are unable to start a conversation at that time:

"I have to go now."
"I can't talk much longer."
"I have someone in my office."
"I was just on my way out the door."
"Can't talk now, I have a houseful of people."

You may even find it necessary to make a list of friends whom you may dearly love but who have a telephone "problem." They engage in monologues and it's rare that you can get off the phone in less than an hour. If you do want to call those kinds of friends, call them when you know they are unable to talk—just to give them a brief message or to stay in touch—or when you have plenty of time that you want to spend on the phone.

You should also consider some of the telephone devices that facilitate effective time management. For example, cordless phones permit you to walk around as you speak. This can be a great time saver if you find yourself saying "I'll call you back" because you need privacy; a cordless phone permits you to find that privacy all the time. Automatic redialing if a number is busy can save time, as can push-button phone dialing versus rotary dials.

You might also consider a speaker phone if there are calls you could handle effectively while doing something else with your hands.

Use the phone creatively and avoid getting a reputation for only calling if you want to "get something" from someone. (One man I know is so used to being called for favors that he answers his phone by asking, "What can I do for you?") Once in a while, call business relations just to say hello. *Listen to your business relation.* You probably won't want to ask in great detail about the golf game last Saturday or the vacation in Spain, and you probably won't want to stay on more than a few minutes, but a sincere "good will" call may be welcome. The "good will call" suggestion, however, should be used with caution; you don't want to get a reputation for being a telephone time waster any more than you want to be known as an opportunist.

Dealing With Visitor Interruptions

In-person "drop in" visitors are as disruptive as telephone visitors who have, in effect, interrupted you with their call. You may be facile at handling both telephone and in-person interruptions but it is usually easier to get off the phone than to turn someone away who is right there in front of you. Without developing the reputation of being cold and aloof, you do want to establish rules for those you work with, namely, that drop-in visits should be avoided if possible. Get your co-workers or employees to develop the habit of calling first. (In some work situations this is impossible since you may work side by side.)

One technique to discourage drop-in visitors at the office, at least temporarily, is to have an established "quiet hour." You might put a sign on your door, "Do not disturb," or just let it be known that you are unavailable for one or more specific hours each day.

If drop-in visitors cannot be handled in other ways, try to deal with the immediate situation and get them out of your office as quickly as possible. Some executives purposely avoid having a chair in their office other than their own; discomfort (and the awkwardness of just standing there) may push visitors out faster than your words. If your drop-in visitor does not get the hint, especially if you have another appointment, come right out and say so. Obviously, if the drop-in visitor is your boss, more tact may be required to get him out, without encouraging his wrath. You might consider going in to see your boss, on a fixed or flexible basis, so drop-in visits to your office are minimized. In that way you might have more control over the situation, especially if you decide in advance what point or priority project you will be discussing.

If your job depends upon the social relations (and subsequent business) that may result from drop-in visits from customers or clients, such interruptions may not be time wasters for your job. If that is the case, you might, for instance, have a hot pot of coffee "on tap" as well as a comfortable sofa for your uninvited guests.

Each type of visitor interruption will be handled differently. Expected visitor interruptions should be planned for in advance with a written agenda for the meeting; any supporting materials that you will need to show or to distribute should be available.

If the visit is unexpected, you have to determine if it is desirable or intrusive. You could be in the midst of preparing a report for later that afternoon, but if the drop-in visitor is the senior vice president, you might want to stop what you're doing.

Time Off (Vacations, Sick Days, Personal Leave)

The right to shorter hours and longer vacations was achieved through the long efforts of laborers and union members. No one, however, will make you take advantage of this extra time; it's up to you not just to take the time that's coming to you, but to plan the kind of activities that will be personally and professionally rewarding. You might think you're saving money by puttering around the house, rather than going away, or saving time by not going away at all. Those who are self-employed often find it especially difficult to take a vacation; they are afraid that their business will deteriorate in their absence, or they are working on overlapping assignments and are unable to take time off during a project. If you can manage it, at least two weeks a year—two one-week vacations or one two-week vacation—will do wonders for replenishing your work abilities. It will also help you break the routine, focus on your health and emotional well-being, and allow you the time to renew intimate relationships. If you can't get away for that length of time, consider what one advertising executive does. He divides his vacation time up throughout the year taking three- or four-day mini-vacations with his wife, never traveling more than two hours by car from home.

Sick days and personal leave are other potential respites from work that you should use to your best advantage. As you learned in the section on obstacles to effective time management, employers are more sympathetic to absences because of physical ailments than emotional ones. You, however, are the best judge as to whether a day off this week might be to your advantage, and to your employer's.

Efficiency Breaks

Build into your workday the kind of rests that Elton Mayo found improved the efficiency of the workers at the Philadelphia textile mills in the 1920's. As Francis and Milbourn tell it in their text, *Human Behavior in the Work Environment,* after efficiency experts and financial incentives for employees failed to reduce a 250 percent worker turnover rate, Mayo was called in for what became known as "The First Inquiry." Mayo discovered that permitting workers who stood all day to take four brief rest periods increased productivity and caused the turnover rate to drop.

If your effectiveness is improved by the rests you take, you will be saving time by breaking for five minutes, ten minutes, or an hour. Only you can decide if, when, and how long an efficiency break will maximize your results. (Some discretion may be called for in some work settings, since your co-workers or employer might misinterpret your "break" as goofing off.) You might try taking one long break, or several short ones; you might try running at lunchtime, as one lawyer in Washington, D.C., does (it's amazing how many offices now have places to change clothes and shower, if there's no nearby health club or "Y"), or sitting under a tree in the summertime, eating lunch out of a brown paper bag. Think of your body as a clock, and get in touch with the alarms that your body sounds when it's time to break away.

Working With Others

Delegating

Whether you work with others, or alone, delegating can dramatically increase how effectively you manage your time. (If you delegate improperly, it can be an enormous time drain.) Delegating—giving up total control of your work and entrusting certain tasks to others—is hard for some workers, yet the inability to delegate often undermines your own, or your company's, growth and profits.

If you have a problem delegating, try to analyze where it stems from: Do you need to control everything in your work environment? Do you doubt you could hire someone competent? Have you had bad prior experiences with delegating so you are afraid to try it again? Are you fearful someone else can do it better than you?

Effective delegation is a three-step process: decide what you need to assign to others; select the person you will delegate to; design a time-effective plan for review of his actual work and of what tasks he is performing. You might find, for instance, that the secretary you hired to type your correspondence is able to compose your letters as well. Redefining her job will thus free up more of your time. Conversely, you may have thought someone could do a certain job as well as you, but her performance proves otherwise. Redefine her job responsibilities, or hire someone else.

You can delegate to another worker or to a machine, a robot or a word processor, for example, or to a service, such as a printing firm that will do addressing and envelope stuffing. Delegating is not the same thing as passing the buck. You are paying someone to perform some of your tasks to free yourself to perform other, usually more important and specialized, ones.

Company presidents, who started a firm from scratch, may still be fixing machines when their time would be better spent planning and inventing. By contrast, in large bureaucracies, being given the power to delegate is seen as a status symbol; the more people that work for you, the more important you must be. Delegating well can lead to increased efficiency; delegating badly— misusing your power—can lead to poor employee relations. For example, it may be tempting to ask your secretary to play babysitter; in the long run, it may be more efficient to have a student you call on just for that purpose.

Working with Your Superiors

Being overly familiar, or too close-mouthed, can cause problems in working with superiors. If you overinvolve your superiors is what you're doing—at work or in your personal life—you may be wasting valuable time that could be spent actually working, or make your superior feel burdened by your own up-and-down personal affairs (and wondering if you can take care of things). If, by contrast, you fail to keep your boss informed about your work, she may falsely believe you are unproductive. Moderation is the key; you don't want to be "all talk, no action" any more than you want to be "all action, no talk."

Let's say you are in charge of a specialized reference collection maintained in a college library. Although somewhat autonomous, you were hired by the senior librarian, and she wants to be informed of your activities. You could keep her informed by writing a weekly, bi-weekly, or monthly memo. You could decide a more informal approach is what's needed— updating her over coffee or lunch every so often. Unless your superiors issue guidelines on how and when to update them on your work—and often they do not—it is up to you to devise, and follow through on, an effective plan. Even if you decide the more casual approach is what's needed, it should not be casual for *you.*

What about socializing outside of the office? Use your discretion. You may think it would aid your office relationship to meet outside of the job. You may decide it would be best to let your boss make the first move. A circumstance might arise, such as an extra pair of tickets to a concert or sports event that you know he'd enjoy, that would naturally lend itself to after-work socializing. Timing, and the personalities involved, should be taken into account on a job by job, situation by situation basis.

Making the Most of Meetings

The daily, weekly, or monthly meeting can be a notorious time waster. Yet, if used correctly, it can also be a time saver. For example, you can use meetings to learn about your company, or your project, so you become aware of new trends.

Here are some guidelines for conducting meetings:

1. Make sure there is a reason for the meeting and that all those expected to attend have been advised, in writing, of that purpose as well as the time the meeting will start and finish. Stick to the starting time; latecomers will get the point.
2. Prepare a written agenda for the meeting and follow it.
3. Decide in advance if you, or someone you delegate to, will take notes during the meeting. If you decide to tape record the meeting, make provisions for transcribing the tape.
4. Keep discussions to the topic at hand, controlling questions that get off on a tangent.
5. Be certain that by the end of the meeting participants have a sense of accomplishment. Summarize what the meeting achieved, if necessary.
6. Decide in advance if you will follow-up the meeting with a written synopsis of what was accomplished.
7. End on time.
8. Thank participants for attending and advise them if they will receive a written or verbal follow-up. If there will be another meeting, announce when it will take place.

If you have to attend a meeting, avoid saying anything just because you want to brag about the work you're doing, as a way of gaining recognition. If you have something specific to contribute, or a pertinent question to ask, by all means speak up. Make notes in advance so that whether you make a statement or ask a question, you present your ideas or questions succinctly and tactfully.

If you attend conferences, set yourself clear goals. If someone else is sending you there, you may be required to write a report detailing what you gained from it. If you do write such a report, keep it simple and clear. You may want to go on for fifteen pages, but you may be wasting the time of the person who has to read it, and your time in creating such a detailed report. Even if you are not asked to set goals, or to write a report, do it for yourself. *Before attending any meeting or conference, have a clear idea what you want to get out of it.*

Compulsive Talkers

Beware the compulsive talker! Compulsive talkers waste their time, and will gladly waste yours, if you let them. Compulsive talkers take energy away from their work and put it into talking about their work.

If you have a compulsive talking problem, consider maintaining a written daily journal as a way of diverting your output away from those around you. (At the least, you'll be saving *them* time.) Maybe you'll have to talk into a tape recorder just to get over your need to talk compulsively, or seek professional help to find out what motivates the constant chatter.

What's behind compulsive talking? Muriel Schiffman, author of *Self*

Therapy and *Gestalt Self Therapy,* describes two types of compulsive talkers, and their motivations:

1. This talker has a dark secret. Talking in this instance is a red herring, like the mother bird who distracts you and tries to lead you away from the baby birds. . . . He is also trying to atone for years of secrecy by "telling all" now (about something else). . . . This kind of talker is often entertaining, if exhausting.
2. This talker has never had anyone to listen to him at some important period in his life. . . . Since a neurotic is someone who never got what he needed in the beginning, he never learned how to get it. So this deprived talker sets himself up again and again to be rejected; he is very boring.

Is there a cure? Schiffman, who had this problem herself, stopped talking compulsively. How? "I sublimated my pattern by lecturing three nights a week and sometimes, by special invitation, from ten a.m. to six p.m. . . . Eventually, after many, many therapy sessions which uncovered innumerable facets to my unconscious motivations, I lost the desire to lecture at all as well as the craving to talk too much."

Psychologist Albert Ellis, author of dozens of books including *Overcoming Procrastination,* notes, "Compulsive talking usually has one or more irrational ideas that lead individuals to go on talking when they are inappropriate" including these four:

1. "I MUST NOT allow any silences, since other people will think that I am responsible for them and that I am something of an incompetent or idiot. I therefore HAVE to keep filling up these silences."
2. "I MUST show others how great I am and what I have outstandingly done. Therefore, I HAVE to keep talking to show this."
3. "I MUST be in the center of everyone's attention and if I merely listen they will ignore me. I CAN'T STAND being ignored in that fashion."
4. "It is easier for me to talk than to keep still; and I MUST give in to what is easy for me and obtain immediate gratification, even though I neglect others in the process."

Workaholics

Are you a workaholic? In her book, *Workaholics,* psychologist Marilyn Machlowitz describes in detail the signs and symptoms: "They love their work. They *live* their work. And most of them find it very difficult to even leave their work, even in extreme circumstances." Here's a checklist she provides to test whether or not you are a workaholic:*

---

*Reprinted by permission of Marilyn Machlowitz, Ph.D. from *Workaholics* (New York: New American Library).

		Yes	No
1.	Do you get up early, no matter how late you go to bed?	____	____
2.	If you are eating lunch alone, do you read or work while you eat?	____	____
3.	Do you make daily lists of things to do?	____	____
4.	Do you find it difficult to "do nothing"?	____	____
5.	Are you energetic and competitive?	____	____
6.	Do you work on weekends and holidays?	____	____
7.	Can you work anytime and anywhere?	____	____
8.	Do you find vacations hard to take?	____	____
9.	Do you dream of retirement?	____	____
10.	Do you really enjoy your work?	____	____

If you answer "Yes" to eight or more, you may be one too.

Only five percent of the work population has this problem, Machlowitz estimates, but it obviously affects a far greater number since there are numerous others who must work for or live with a workaholic. Strangely enough, workaholics may not necessarily accomplish more than non-workaholics, Machlowitz concludes. In twelve hours they may only do eight hours of work. By focusing on their work, they diminish the energy they can apply in their personal lives, leading to a higher rate of divorce (unless they find other workaholics to live with or very understanding spouses who enjoy being alone when the workaholic is working).

Workaholics are perfectionists and high energy people; being around them, or working for or with them, places demands on others that they may not meet. Like alcoholism, workaholism is a hard addiction to cure. Workaholism is a time waster in disguise. "I use my work to avoid socializing," says Kathy, 32, an analyst for a stockbrokerage firm. Saturday nights, when she might be out on a date, Kathy is home, rereading financial newspapers. The basis of workaholism is the mismanagement of work and personal time. Workaholics, oblivious of the schedules that others adhere to, may even be found working on Christmas Day—along with their dutiful employees.

Improving Communication at Work

Communication in work situations may involve two persons (dyadic), three persons (triadic), four or more persons (social network). There are elements that are unique to each type of interaction. A dyad, say you and your boss, has the potential for greater intimacy (and confidentiality). It also is less secure since it depends on both members for its maintenance but only one for its dissolution. A triad is easier to maintain since the third member serves to perpetuate the group. It is, however, less intimate since secrecy is less assured than in a dyad. A network of four or five, such as a typing pool, has the potential for hundreds of interrelationships. Relationships may be more superficial than in a dyad or triad, but easier still to maintain.

Communication at work may be improved by understanding the nature of your work relationships (whether they are dyadic, triadic, or networks), basics about communication skills, and certain complexities of social relationships that may inhibit good communication. For example, the self-fulfilling prophesy means that the perception you have of yourself may become true. Thus if you see yourself as someone who is competent and able to relate well at the office, it may become true. Conversely, if you see yourself as someone who has trouble communicating with your superiors and is insecure, that may become true. Similarly, if you define your co-worker as difficult to talk to, and work with, your definition of your co-worker may become true if you behave in a manner that inspires him to respond in that mode.

Obviously a good self-image will enhance your relationships and, in turn, your communication at the office. One way to improve your self-image is to create a progressive spiral. In *Dyadic Communication,* William W. Wilmot describes how that works: ". . . the actions of the individual supply a multiplier effect in reinforcement. The better you do, the more worthwhile you feel; the more worthwhile you feel, the better you do." Two communication inhibitors that Wilmot cautions against are paradoxes and double binds. A paradox is a contradictory statement such as the following:

> Ignore this sign

A double bind is a type of paradox in which a nonverbal message contradicts a verbal one. For example, you come into the office looking tired and overworked. When your boss asks if you've been working too hard you answer, "No, I've never been more rested." Your appearance contradicts your statement and places your boss in a double bind.

You cannot control how your boss, subordinates, or co-workers talk to you but you can control your own verbal and nonverbal behavior. Since it is a fact of interpersonal relationships that communication is usually reciprocal—people respond to you as you respond to them and vice versa—through your own behavior you do have some control. If you have a good self-image and avoid paradoxes and double binds, you have a better chance of inspiring similar communication with those you work with.

Since communication is reciprocal, you may wish to avoid telling your boss or subordinates information that it would be inappropriate for them to tell you in kind. Take the long view of your work relationships rather than trying to come on too strong and too fast.

WORK/SCHOOL-RELATED GOALS

Long-range Planning

People who fail to manage their time efficiently are unable to set and maintain long-range goals. They let the daily ups and downs of their jobs interfere with accomplishing their primary goals. Obviously it is hard to break a long-range goal down into small steps—and stick to those steps in a way which will eventually lead to the desired end. A secretary may find that just by performing the tasks that her boss demands she is able to complete her daily jobs. She may not, however, be thinking about how to become a more valuable worker so she gets a raise (or a promotion).

Consider your long-range career goals. Where do you want to be ten years from now? five years? one year? How about your short-term goals? Where do you want to be next month? next week? tomorrow?

Starting to think in terms of objectives that you wish to accomplish will make it easier for you to prioritize what you do. Some experts feel that few people are able to handle more than three work-related goals simultaneously. (Some people find they can only handle *one!*) Within each goal, however, there may be dozens, hundreds, or thousands of small steps that you will have to take. Jack, for example, has been studying at night for his Master's degree. Jack refuses to set a target date for completing his degree. It drains his energy to think about school, so he fails to marshal his resources, finish up, and be free forever.

Progress Reports

Where people who manage their time poorly need the most help is in setting realistic *daily* goals. Breaking a large task up into daily tasks is the foundation of good time management. If you feel overwhelmed by how large your goal is—writing a book, getting a degree, giving a speech, completing a study, selling x number of tractors, or designing an employee manual—break it down into daily goals. You may find that by tackling, and achieving, a manageable task—"Today I will call seven sales prospects" or "Today I will read sixty pages in the textbook"—you will feel a sense of accomplishment. Reward yourself for achieving that goal and use the remaining time to achieve another goal (or improve what you've already done).

Progress reports may be only for your boss; a personal progress report might give you the daily feedback that you need to manage your time better. Jerry, an aspiring novelist, bought a diary solely to list the activities he accomplished that day, even if it was just "Spent three hours thinking about the plot of my novel." In that way, he began to see that the time he thought he was wasting—because he didn't have any manuscript pages to show for it— he actually had used wisely. Even though it took him two years to finish the novel, entering into his diary "Wrote twenty pages today" made the task more manageable than focusing on "How am I ever going to write four hundred enthralling pages?"

Consider creating or purchasing daily progress sheets to keep track of your accomplishments. Here's a sample of an activity sheet with some of the categories filled in:

Work Sheet

Hours	Activity	Date _Tuesday, June 2_
		Accomplished
9 a.m.–11 a.m.	Phone calls	Accepted lecture. Returned calls from yesterday.
11 a.m.–12	Correspondence	Answered 5 letters.
12–1 p.m.	Lunch	Read *Wall Street Journal.*
1–3 p.m.	Meeting	Very little!
3–5 p.m.	Dictating	Notes on meeting.
5–7 p.m.	Commuting	Read magazines.

Your activity/accomplishment log need not be divided up by time periods; one man has his day divided up into these four categories: Work; Chores; Exercise; and Relaxation. Within his own categories, he lists what he's accomplishing that day.

It's important not just to do what you have to do right now, but to follow up on what happens with that project you started, the idea you submitted to your boss, or the memo you distributed. Do you check up on projects, memos, or unanswered telephone calls? Do you let too much time—or not enough—elapse between starting and completing a job-related function? Are you projecting an image that will further, or hinder, your career?

In *Getting Things Done,* Edwin C. Bliss advises that right after a project has been completed, especially if you've been dissatisfied with the outcome, write yourself a brief appraisal. Note what you learned from that project. Date it and keep it for later review. If you fail to make notes at the time the experience is fresh in your mind, you'll miss one of the best self-teaching experiences that you'll have.

Measuring Your Success

The Hawthorne Effect, discovered by Elton Mayo when he was conducting an experiment on the effect of levels of illumination on worker productivity at an electric company in the late 1920's and early 1930's, shows why measuring your success is important. Mayo found that workers in the control group (who did not have any changes made in their lighting) showed increased productivity; at the same time, whether lights were dimmed or brightened, those in the experimental group showed increased productivity. The phenomenon, known as the Hawthorne Effect, meant this: just the act of being studied or measured led to increased productivity.

You can draw your own conclusions as to whether this increase was due to the need to impress the researcher (employed by management) or because of the favorable human response to being noticed and cared about. Generally, you are not evaluated daily by others. Is there a way you can employ the Hawthorne Effect to your advantage? Daily logs will help; no one can observe you more intimately than you, yourself.

There are many ways of measuring success—in dollars and cents, by promotions, or in public recognition. Whatever you decide are your measures for success, make them concrete so you'll know when you've achieved them. Maybe it's just getting home by six o'clock. "Becoming president of the company," "Not taking work on vacation with me," or "Having something to talk about besides football the next time I see my friends" are some others.

Managing your time at work well means figuring out what you have to do, and doing it, as quickly and effectively as possible.

Handling correspondence, telephone calls, vacations, and all the other necessary parts of your job enable you to accomplish your work-related goals; they are not, however, your ultimate goal. Putting in more time for your work may ultimately be your aim, but most of us want to put in quality time, and to achieve quality work, not simply work harder at it.

In the next chapter we'll look at creative ways of handling a certain kind of work few can escape, namely housework.

TERMS

workaholism	self-fulfilling prophesy	double bind
word processor	flexitime	paradox
dyad	The Hawthorne Effect	
network	triad	

REFERENCES

BLANK, RAYMOND. *Playing the Game: A Psychopolitical Strategy for Your Career.* New York: William Morrow and Company, Inc., 1981.

BLISS, EDWIN C. *Getting Things Done.* New York: Bantam Books, 1976.

FRANCIS, G. JAMES, and GENE MILBOURN, JR. *Human Behavior in the Work Environment: A Managerial Perspective.* Santa Monica, Calif.: Goodyear Publishing Company, Inc., 1980. A textbook based on the behavioral approach to work, which "assumes that people can contribute more to an organization than just the performance of a specific task."

GABARRO, JOHN J., and JOHN P. KOTTER. "Managing Your Boss," *Harvard Business Review* (January–February 1980):92–100.

KORDA, MICHAEL. *Power!* New York: Ballantine Books, 1975. A self-help book, laden with examples, with the purpose of telling you "how to use, recognize and live with power."

———. *Success!* New York: Ballantine Books, 1977. A well-written, popular book on understanding the business world and how to conquer it.

KOTTER, JOHN P. "What Effective General Managers Really Do," *Harvard Business Review* (November—December 1982):156–67.

MACHLOWITZ, MARILYN. *Workaholics; Living With Them, Working With Them.* Reading, Mass: Addison-Wesley Publishing Company, 1980.

McWILLIAMS, PETER A. *The Word Processing Book: A Short Course In Computer Literacy.* Los Angeles, Calif.: Prelude Press, 1982.

ONCKEN, WILLIAM, JR., and DONALD L. WASS. "Management Time: Who's Got the Monkey?," *Harvard Business Review* (November–December 1974): 75–80.

RONEN, SIMCHA. *Flexible Working Hours: An Innovation in the Quality of Work Life.* New York: McGraw-Hill, Inc., 1981.

SCHIFFMAN, MURIEL. *Gestalt Self Therapy.* Berkeley, Calif.: Bookpeople, 1971.

———. *Self Therapy.* Berkeley, Calif.: Bookpeople, 1967.

WILMOT, WILLIAM W. *Dyadic Communication,* 2nd edition. Reading, Mass.: Addison-Wesley Publishing Company, 1979.

ZELKO, HAROLD P. *Successful Conference and Discussion Techniques.* New York: McGraw-Hill Book Company, Inc., 1957.

EXERCISES

1. Write down your "ideal" workday. What are your fantasies, dreams, and visions of you as an efficient worker? How much time is spent getting

dressed? Commuting to the office? Working at home? How many coffee breaks? How long for lunch? The average phone call? Write a list, or a paragraph, about that ideal workday.

2. Think about the work habits of a few people that you know intimately. Try to imagine how they spend their time, and see if you think they are managing their time well or poorly. It may be easier to see time being wasted by others than by yourself. Plan how you would restructure their workday to increase their efficiency.

3. Set one goal for improving your time at work. Concentrate on that one goal before you move on to another one. Don't tackle too many goals at once! Achieve that one goal; the success you feel will inspire you to go on to your next one. Here are possible work-related improvements:

>Lengthen or shorten your lunchtime.
>Plan a vacation this year you will really enjoy.
>Find a certain time each day (or each week) to keep up with correspondence.
>Delegate a task you thought only you could do.
>Limit the time you spend on the phone with personal calls.
>Decrease, or increase, the number of work-related publications that you receive or read.

5
Saving Time on Household Chores

A fool and his time are soon parted.
ANONYMOUS

Whether you live alone in a studio apartment in Chicago, with your mate in an attached house in Washington, D.C., or with your two children and spouse in a suburban ranch-style home in Denver, home is where you spend, and perhaps waste, most of your time. Even if you're "out every night," or you do a great deal of traveling, you spend more time in your home than any other one place. We think of work as something to go to, and home the place you come from.

At work, maintenance chores are usually taken care of by janitors, laundry services, cleaning personnel, cafeteria workers, or secretaries. All you usually have to do is keep your desktop and other workspace neat. At home, maintenance chores, depending upon whom you live with and your economic level, may include such time-consuming responsibilities as food shopping, cooking, cleaning, doing the laundry, entertaining, decorating, repairing minor appliances, acquiring and maintaining clothing, purchasing furniture and electronics equipment, and gardening. For most, the skills needed for maintaining a household have been acquired haphazardly by "on the job" training, aided or hindered by observations of others (usually one's own parents), reading books and magazines, or taking an occasional course.

This chapter will discuss some time-effective strategies for necessary chores—food shopping, cleaning, washing clothes, vacuuming—tasks that almost everyone faces. Unless you are that very rare individual who loves housework, doing these jobs faster will be a welcome time saver. Not surprisingly, Ann Oakley, who studied how London housewives behave, reported in *The Sociology of Housework* that housework was the aspect of married life that the women she interviewed liked least. For the forty women closely studied by Oakley, the housewives had an average work week of 77 hours (versus the average 40 hour worker's week). As the number of children increased, so did the number of hours at their job. Interestingly, the one woman in her sample with a full-time job outside the home spent only 48 hours doing house-related work. Perhaps housework (including shopping and childrearing activities), like other tasks, will expand to fill the number of available hours—unless you have a plan.

With married women comprising more than fifty percent of the work force, finding ways to speed up household chores is a necessity. Men are pitching in—to be sure, some more than others—and they also need ways to get the job done as quickly, and as pleasantly, as possible. If you live alone, housekeeping chores are all yours; you'll probably want to do them quickly so you have more time for other things.

Some time wasters discussed in Chapter Two also interfere with effective time management in the home. For example, the perfectionist may spend waking hours cleaning, puttering, and worrying about every minor detail in the home. Unless you are willing to devote that kind of full-time attention to your home, you might consider modifying your standards of cleanliness and orderliness. If you've been knocking yourself out dusting every other day, you might try doing it once a week and see if it makes a difference to anyone (including you).

Fear of failure or success may also be a factor in taking too long with housework. If a woman is afraid of competing in the job world (and sees it as a man's world), she may stretch out the time housekeeping takes to justify her not getting a job. She may fear competing at an outside job and use housework to keep busy so she doesn't run the risk of any actual or fantasized repercussions.

Housework also provides instant gratification: results of your efforts are clearly visible when a sink full of dishes disappears or a room is transformed by your purchases. Success in a career may not be so readily apparent. At work, responsibilities may be vague; at home, not only are the responsibilities ongoing and consistent—beds always need to be made, towels need to be washed again—but once a homemaker sets up a ritual, all that's required is a steady labor.

There is no single time-effective way to do household chores. Some find a fixed schedule best; others prefer to work *ad hoc.* One retired man jogs after he puts in the casserole he's made for dinner. By the time he returns, his wife is back from her full-time job, and dinner's ready. What matters is having a system that works for you so that household chores do not consume time that could be spent in a more meaningful way.

BECOMING ORGANIZED AT HOME

Obviously it is easier to organize an apartment or a home if you have just moved in. Everything is still in boxes, you put up those extra shelves in the pantry, you decide what will go where in each of the closets, you categorize your books as you put them back on the shelves, and so forth. Most of us are already living somewhere, however, and we would like to *re*organize our living space without having to move out.

You will save time, and enjoy an uncluttered and pleasant environment, if you start organizing your home, one room or one project at a time. Divide your home up in a way that will make organizing or reorganizing it easiest for you. The most obvious ways of approaching this would be—

1. By project (e.g., closets, drawers, shelves, etc.)
2. By room (e.g., living room, dining room, kitchen, etc.)

Consider starting from your front door and working your way through your apartment or home. First, concentrate on what shows as soon as you enter your home. Having organized your hallway, living room, or guest bathroom will reinforce the initial expenditure of time and effort.

Investing time in creating order will save you countless hours of time for a long time to come.

Second, tackle the more challenging "hidden" areas of disorder, like inside the closets and drawers. Only you, and those with whom you live, will benefit from these organizational efforts. The payoff will be even greater than the compliments received from guests who are impressed by your neat living room.

Systematically organizing your home a room, or an area, at a time may work best for you. That approach allows you to fully explore all the needs that you or your family want that area or room to fulfill. Example: Is your living room where you want to have a study corner for handling paperwork or is it just a place to entertain? Your answer to that question will help you to reorganize your space accordingly. Your dresser drawers can have dividers, so that socks, shirts, undergarments, underwear, and other everyday pieces of clothing are easily organized (and located). For women, a lingerie chest, with small, multiple drawers, is a useful way to organize such small items as pocketbooks, gloves, summer tops, and scarves, in addition to lingerie and undergarments.

Consider organizing the kitchen. You want to have most accessible to you those materials that you need and use most frequently. (This is based on the same Active and Inactive organizing principle that you have applied to your files.) You can keep in another part of the kitchen, or even in another room, those materials that you do not use regularly. You may decide your kitchen needs a waste can at both ends, to cut down on unnecessary walking.

Proximity, especially in the kitchen, will save you minutes each day, and hours each week, in food preparation, serving, clean-up, and in general household maintenance.

It is useful in organizing each area in your home to think of each part of the whole as important in and of itself. For example, the way you organize inside the refrigerator and inside the freezer can save you as much time as how you organize your cabinets and drawers.

Keep in mind all the organizing principles that you learned in Chapter Three including the following time-saving rules:

Frequently used items should be kept in accessible places.

Have a place for everything.

Eliminate clutter.

Periodically go through all your possessions and give away, throw out, or rearrange to suit your current needs.

Create and follow "to do" lists for your home-related obligations.

Delegate whenever possible.

Household Responsibilities

Even if you hire someone to organize your home, you will probably have to do the day-to-day maintenance. Everyday maintenance, however, like making the beds or preparing and serving dinner, is often easier to find time for than seasonal timely chores like cleaning the windows, washing the car, or planting the flowers and vegetables. Whether you live alone, with a roommate, or with children, consider delegating specific tasks to others. If those you live with will not, or cannot, do these chores, you might, if you can afford it, consider delegating some of them to paid workers, e.g., window washers, cleaning ladies, someone to do the laundry. If you cannot afford to pay someone for doing those heavy household tasks, consider what skills you can offer or barter in exchange for someone else doing the housework you despise.

If you have a roommate of the same sex, dividing up the household chores may be easier than if you are married. (Socialized expectations about the wife's role in housekeeping complicates what a woman or a man "should" do even if both are working full-time.) For same-sex roommates, make a list of housekeeping tasks and simply decide whose job it is— permanently or an alternating basis.

If you are a parent, have you considered what responsibilities your child can handle even at a very young age? In addition to "feeding my doll, playing with my sister, and being a good girl," a four-year-old girl in

Massachusetts gave a list of household responsibilities that are hers alone or that she helps with: clean up my toys; dress myself; feed the fish; rake the leaves; wash the car; make my bed; wash up; and let Daddy sleep late on Sunday. Giving children household responsibilities, and increasing those responsibilities as they grow, takes up less of your time than trying to do it all and complaining about your martyrdom.

HOUSEHOLD PROJECTS

Decorating

Whether you are decorating an apartment or home for the first time, or renovating one or more rooms where you've been living for a while, *decorate for efficiency as well as comfort and appearance.* It's best to take things one step at a time. In a new home, you can do one project at a time (refinishing all the floors, painting, building wall units, for example); if you're renovating, you may more readily do it a room at a time. In both situations, follow the same time management rules that you've been learning: *Set your priorities and then, in an orderly fashion, go about carrying them out.*

How do you proceed? Do you hire a decorator? Do you try to do it yourself? Hiring a decorator may save you time, but it will be more expensive. You may also lose the creative pleasure of carrying your own ideas through to completion. If you select, trust, and hire a decorator, he can supervise the changes, while you do something else. Hiring a decorator is not simply a matter of finding a name in the telephone directory. You'll need to visit homes he's decorated to see if his concepts and yours are compatible; you'll need to talk with him; you'll need to provide ideas, consider his suggestions, and approve a proposed budget and the completed work. You certainly don't want to hand a check to a decorator and thereafter live in his or her concept of "home."

If major purchases are involved, you should have any necessary structural changes (putting up or tearing down walls/windows/doors, sanding and staining floors, painting, scraping old wallpaper and repapering) completed before the new or recovered furniture arrives. Furniture, rugs, and even houseplants can be damaged by any processes involving caustic chemicals, paints, sanding, or dust.

It may be cost-ineffective to do major work yourself. Unless you are a professional and know what you're doing, these are complex tasks, both to learn and to carry out properly. In addition, you will have to rent or purchase all the equipment necessary to complete the job. Finally, if you botch the job, you'll have to pay for professionals to undo your mess, and then redo things correctly. You have to weigh the benefits of doing it yourself (possible lower expenditures and a feeling of pride in having done it by yourself) versus the negative aspects (extra time, and ultimately, cost involved, and possible frustration).

Painting, Floor Coverings, Repairs, and Other Improvements

Before you completely redecorate, consider repainting. It may save you many hours of needless redecorating, while still achieving a "new" look. Try a dramatically different color—changing from white to powder blue—using another color for accent (on baseboards, moldings, window trims, or cabinets). A new color will change a room or, as designer Mary Gilliatt, author of *The Decorating Book,* puts it: "Color can transform a home more quickly and cheaply than any other decorational device, disguising faults and altering the whole feeling of a space in as short a time as it takes to paint or cover the walls."

Painting "seems" to require more muscle than skill and, if you have the time and the tools, you may completely paint the inside of a house (and perhaps the outside too). George, 67, a retired salesman who has painted all the homes he has lived in, says: "With today's new latex paints, almost anyone can paint a room without any real difficulty." Remember, however, that more tricky points are likely to arise if you tackle outside painting: vagaries of weather and use of high ladders, for starters. There are a few considerations about hiring a painter versus doing it yourself:

1. Will you do a better job than the painter? (Sometimes, when a landlord provides the painter, the paint used is of such poor quality, and the paint job so sloppy, that you are better off doing it yourself.)
2. If you choose to hire a painter, can you select the brand of paint that you want? If you supply your own paint, will the fee be discounted? To save time on household maintenance, and to lengthen the time between paint jobs, you'll want paint that will allow your walls to be kept clean easily. There are basically two types of paint: oil-based alkyds and water-based latex. Both types of paint are available in three finishes: flat, semi-gloss, and gloss. Oil-based alkyds are more durable, but take longer on application to dry. They are also messier and require paint thinner for cleaning brushes and spills. Alkyds are recommended for kitchens, bathrooms, and frequently used doors. Water-based latex paints dry faster and are easier to use, but do not wash off as well; they are usually used for the walls and ceilings in living rooms and bedrooms.
3. Do you have the time to carefully prepare your valued possessions as well as to cover floors and windows, so that paint splatters will not ruin anything? (Do not rely solely on painters' drop cloths.)
4. Will someone be home to supervise the painting?
5. Can you paint the walls or selected smaller rooms yourself, and have some of the rooms, and/or the ceilings, done professionally?
6. You might finish painting one room, and then move furniture and valuables into that room, safe from the painting going on everywhere else.

7. Have you thought of installing wall coverings that require less upkeep (wood paneling, mosaic tiling, wallpaper, fabric, etc.)? Easy-to-clean ceramic tiles may be used in areas other than the kitchen or bathroom. Wood paneling requires less maintenance than painted walls, and has added insulating and acoustic benefits, but also added cost. Wallpapers are available in a variety of colors, textures, and patterns; vinyl wallpapers are easier to maintain since they may be scrubbed and washed.

There are wide choices today in floor coverings, including wall-to-wall carpeting, area rugs, wood (parquet, strip, and plank), tile, or vinyl. Your decision should be based on taste and style, durability, and cost. Ceramic tile, which is a very durable and easy-to-maintain floor covering, may be noisy to walk on and cold to bare feet. Place an area rug on top to offset those disadvantages. Vinyl floors, available in individual squares or in sheets, is less expensive than ceramic tiles, quieter, but less durable. Wall-to-wall carpeting, a good insulator against footsteps, scraping chairs, or the cold, may be hard to maintain. It is also easier to pick up and move carpeting, from room to room or to another home. Consider a room's functions when you choose the type of carpet (wool, a synthetic blend, or an industrial type) and the color (dark or lighter shades or patterns). A beige wool rug with a medium pile may be fine for an infrequently used living room but it could become a worn and dirty mess if installed in a heavily trafficked hallway.

The same rule about hiring professionals versus doing it yourself applies to repairs and miscellaneous improvements: Do it yourself only if you are qualified, through self-study or courses, and if you have the time and interest. Get an estimate on the cost of a new item before you invest the time and money in repairing it yourself. You may find that it is cheaper to buy a new one than to have it repaired.

HOUSEHOLD MAINTENANCE

Cleaning, Laundry, and Errands

The best overall time saver in your home or apartment is this: *Make it maintenance-free.* Invest the extra time and money to eliminate as many ongoing cleaning demands as you can: tweed rugs camouflage dirt better than solid ones; high-gloss enamel paint in the kitchen or children's rooms easily wipes clean; durable furniture does not readily show or accept stains, and needs only occasional vacuuming; plastic tablecloths are easier to care for than cloth ones; carefully planned storage units ensure that everything has a place, and tidying up is minimized.

In *Is There Life After Housework?*, Don Aslett, president of a cleaning business that he founded, gives this advice about making your home or apartment as maintenance-free as possible:

> . . . Work can be lessened, and time saved, by good maintenance planning and decorating. . . . A bathroom is no place for elaborate bookcases, statues, or other unmaintainable furniture and fixtures. Keep in mind the following:
> 1. Will it clean?
> 2. Will it last?
> 3. Is it usable?

Create a housekeeping time inventory, and base it on the time you *think* you spend in performing each of the major household chores. Then, time yourself and write down the *actual* time spent. You won't feel "on top of things" unless you know how much time you really need/spend, and can allot that much, with a little extra for the "anything that can go wrong" syndrome.

Another way to save lots of time is to purchase six months' worth of household items—especially toiletries and nonperishable maintenance supplies—and have them on hand. It is annoying, and inefficient, to have to run to the corner store just to buy a light bulb. In order to stock up, you've got to have an organized plan of what you need. A good rule of thumb is to replenish when you have only a week's supply left. Shopping in quantity, and in advance, also allows you to get the best prices. For storage, use the active/inactive principle: most frequently used items most accessible, back-up items nearby, and surplus items still available but not "at hand."

Another time saver is to compile an up-to-date list of those services and professionals that you may need in the course of maintaining a residence. Sorting out scraps of paper, and eliminating searches through the phone book, will save you time; it will also ease those frenzied moments just after the pipe bursts and you need a plumber quickly.

Some homemakers find it faster to do their household chores before leaving for their office; it sets a time limit on a limitless task and also enables them to look forward to chore-less evenings and weekends. Gloria, a 40-year-old beautician, uses Saturdays from 9 a.m. to 2 p.m. to do the week's cleaning. Carol, whose four children are grown and on their own, does her cleaning in the evenings, from 9 to 11 p.m., after she has prepared, served, and cleaned up dinner. She prefers to do cleaning on weekday nights, since she works full-time, so the weekends, her husband's and her only time to socialize, are clear.

Make sure that the appliances you use for cleaning are the best you can afford: a vacuum cleaner without enough suction power or the appropriate accessories can prolong that chore unnecessarily. If you decide to purchase, or replace, new appliances for cleaning, first check the latest *Consumer Reports*

Buying Guide Issue, or ask friends what specific brand names and models they are using and if they are pleased.

To save time on errands, make use of as many pick-up and delivery services as you can. If you have to do it in person, try to do several chores at the same time—leaving some days completely errand-free. For example, pick up your shoes, dry cleaning, and the day's newspapers in one trip. Laundry should not be the time-consuming task that some make it out to be. If you have enough reserve items so that you don't have to do laundry every third day, you can stall for a week, or even two weeks. It takes about the same time (if sufficient machines are available) to do five loads as to do two. If you have a machine in your home, let the machine run while you do other things. Clock exactly how long the washing machine and/or dryer take so you can use that time productively doing something else. You might also consider service laundromats that will do the work for you.

Household Directories/Records

It will save lots of time in the long run if you have an effective record-keeping system in your home, whether for household financial matters (income, expenses, tax deductions, contributions, etc.) or for health matters (names of physicians and past medical problems, name of any medication currently being taken, dates of vaccinations, etc.). There are inexpensive record-keeping systems you can purchase (from labeled envelopes in record folders to entire books giving you step-by-step instructions for completing and following through on a budget).

An important consideration is: *Enter the information as soon as it is available or it will not be readily available when needed.* To keep track of expenses, consider a pocket-sized expense record that you can carry around with you, right in your wallet or pocketbook, so that you can enter information as you go along. One way to keep track of physician visits is to schedule all semi-annual and annual check-ups during the same two-week period each year. Then, when that time of year comes around, you know it's time to go for your check-ups (such as the dentist, the eye doctor, the gynecologist, the internist).

Create a list of personal records (credit card numbers, driver's license number, etc.), and keep it in a safe place (not your wallet). Also create a list of key names and phone numbers that is kept up to date, and in an accessible place, to facilitate contacting any of these services or professionals quickly, such as fire and police department, hospitals, physicians, etc.

Food: Preparation, Shopping, Storage, and Cleanup

Food is one of the necessities in life and, if you are not organized about it, one of the biggest time drainers—even several hours a day. If you have been solely responsible for all the meals, you might consider weaning your family away from this dependency with one or both of the following ideas: have a "fend for yourself night," or ask your spouse if just one night a week, dinner could be his or her responsibility. You might also consider doing all your cooking for the weekend on Fridays—preparing tuna fish, egg salad, shrimp salad, and pot roast, for example—so that you can have a completely non-cooking weekend. If you've been cooking every night, you might try ordering in or eating out once a week, if the budget can bear it. Remember, eating out may not save time—you've got to get to the restaurant, order, eat, and get back—but at least you don't have to think about what you'll prepare, or do the cooking, serving, and cleaning up afterwards.

Saving time in the kitchen requires planning—you need a clear idea of what you're going to do, and what equipment or ingredients you'll need, as well as directions for carrying out that plan. One married woman of sixty-five (who worked full-time even while her three children were small) never starts a dish until she has all the ingredients on hand and placed in front of her on the kitchen counter.

Follow the suggestions at the beginning of this chapter for organizing your kitchen. You might also consider having close at hand a chart, such as the one in *The Household Handbook,* listing the use for each spice and condiment. You might also find a slow cooker a time-saving device that enables you to prepare dinner the night before, or in the morning before work, and to have it cook all day and be ready and waiting when you return home. With a slow cooker and an oven/broiler (for fast and simple broiled meats and oven-cooked poultry, fish, and meat), you're all set. Another time-saving cooking device is an electric rice cooker, available in several sizes so you can make, and keep warm, enough rice for one to thirty persons. Those busy housemakers with microwave ovens tell me that they are fabulous time savers when it comes to reheating leftovers or heating frozen foods. Conventional ovens seem to be favored for preparing dishes from scratch. If you do a lot of baking and chopping, food processors may save you time mixing dough or grinding large quantities of food. For chopping up vegetables, however, the consensus seems to be that a sharp knife and your hands are the fastest method. By contrast, electric mixers and juicers are faster than comparable equipment relying on arm power.

Consider getting a large supply of different-sized freezer-type plastic containers so that when you do cook, you can make double or triple the quantity of any main course, and freeze the remainder for later defrosting and serving. Another time saver is having a meal-sealing procedure for freezing foods. You can purchase an inexpensive kit that allows you to seal fresh foods or prepared meals in plastic bags. Since you can use different-sized bags, or cut the plastic to fit the size of the food you are storing, the food takes up less space in the freezer. When you need it, these frozen bags of food can be quickly warmed up in the bag in a pot of boiling water, thus eliminating dirty pots that take time to wash. If you bake, you should consider freezing a second, or even a third cake, for later defrosting. You may even find it pays to buy an extra freezer to get additional cold storage capacity.

When shopping and storing food, keep in mind the storage capacity of perishables, frozen and canned foods. Consider stocking dehydrated and freeze-dried foods, which will last even longer than canned goods. (Most wet-packed canned goods have a shelf life of six months to a year and a half if stored at a temperature of 0–70 degrees; shelf life is cut in half with higher temperatures.)

To save time in food shopping, keep a pad and pencil in your kitchen to jot down items as you realize you need them. You might also create a master grocery list, and have a quantity of blank forms on hand, bringing a completed form with you on your trip to the supermarket.

Make a plan—decide on a menu, whether for breakfast, lunch, or dinner—and execute your plan as quickly as possible. The biggest time waster in the kitchen is to select ingredients willy-nilly and try to pull a meal together. Unless you're a "natural" cook, try to have at least ten or twenty recipes memorized or nearby that you and your family enjoy. Also have close at hand cookbooks and clipped recipes that you plan to try out. For those nights you just don't want to take the time to cook, and you can't get other family members to do it for you, have a list of restaurants or food services that you can call to "order in" dinner. If it doesn't offend your environmental sympathies, consider having a stock of paper plates and cups on hand for those times when you just don't want to take the time to do the dishes.

TERMS

oil-based alkyd paint   slow cooker   water-based latex paint

REFERENCES

ASLETT, DON. *Is There Life After Housework?* Cincinnati, Ohio: Writer's Digest Books, 1981.

BURGESS, CONSTANCE. "Keeping Records: What to Discard," reprinted from *Handbook for the Home* (U.S. Department of Agriculture). Washington, D.C.: U.S. Government Printing Office, 1976. A short guide on which family-type records are important documents to save, and which ones you can toss out.

THE EDITORS OF CONSUMER GUIDE. *Consumer Reports Buying Guide,* updated annually. Mount Vernon, N.Y.: Consumers Union of United States, Inc.

————. *Do It Yourself and Save Money!* New York: Harper & Row Publishers, 1980. How to do 500 plus household projects, from unsticking a window and covering an air conditioner to building a partition wall and laying a tile floor. Illustrated.

GILLIATT, MARY. *The Decorating Book.* New York: Pantheon Books, 1981.

HELOISE. *Hints from Heloise.* New York: Avon Books, 1980. A collection of helpful hints by syndicated columnist Heloise; covers everything from cooking, laundry, and sewing to desk work, grooming, and wardrobe tips.

MEADOWBROOK REFERENCE GROUP. *The Household Handbook.* Depphaven, Minn.: Meadowbrook Press.

OAKLEY, ANN. *The Sociology of Housework.* New York: Pantheon Books, 1974.

ROMBAUER, IRMA S., and MARION ROMBAUER BECKER. *Joy of Cooking,* revised edition. New York: New American Library, 1973, 1931. The one illustrated comprehensive cookbook that no kitchen should be without. Contains basic information, as well as over 4,300 recipes.

RUFF, HOWARD J. *How to Prosper During the Coming Bad Years: A Crash Course in Personal Survival.* New York: Times Books, 1979.

EXERCISES

1. Do an efficiency check of your apartment or home, keeping in mind all of the household chores you must perform. Compare the way you do them now to an ideal method or schedule. Try implementing one or more time-saving techniques suggested in this chapter.

2. Are there household chores that you could be delegating to family members or professional service people? Try delegating one task each week for the next few weeks; if you live alone, hire help for some tasks.

3. Create seven dinner menus, including new recipes you'd like to try. After you've written down the menus, list *all* the ingredients that you will need. Check your supplies and note any that you have to buy.

4. Create the plan you will follow for crash time-saving (e.g. ordering in, letting chores go for a while, having nonperishable foods on hand for easy meals) so when you need undistracted time, you can manage more easily.

6
Improving Your Personal Time Management

Wherein lies happiness?

JOHN KEATS
(*Endymion*)

Personal time management means making time for whatever you enjoy: family members, friends, bowling, playing video games, meditating, knitting, watching TV, reading a novel, writing one, or even working eighteen hours a day. It's up to you how you want to spend that time, and with whom. Daily jogging may be a joy to one man; another may prefer to bask on a beach. One couple fills their weekends with the theater and concerts; another couple dances the night away. Some may need to spend their free time like one man, who does "absolutely nothing" at least ten hours a week, "just sitting there, possibly thinking about something, possibly not," as he puts it. This chapter won't tell you what to do with your personal time; it will, however, help you to find ways to follow through on your needs and wishes.

As with time management on the job, personal time management is taken for granted unless something unexpected occurs. Then, you highlight the "if onlys" or vow to live differently from now on—your grandmother dies and you wish you had gotten to know her better; your spouse tells you she wants a divorce because you've neglected her for the last two years (and she's found someone who hasn't); your physician advises you to relax more or you're headed for a heart attack; your best friend moves away and you feel lonely; a co-worker invites you to the amateur play she's in and you realize you've always wanted to act in your spare time.

Perhaps the ones who will find it hardest to improve their personal time are those who ask, "What free time?", unaware that most of their life is free time. Whatever the current state of your time outside of work or school, even if you feel you have "none," read on.

RECREATION

It is not surprising to find that in a society that applauds accomplishment, doing something just for its own sake occupies a low priority. You don't go running because you enjoy it, you do it to exercise the cardiovascular system. You don't join civic groups because you like to be around people, but to make contacts that will help your career. You don't sew because it's fun, but to save money. However, if you value yourself, and your own happiness, you'll want to make the most of your personal time. It is sad that personal time—the time we truly do have more control over—can be less satisfying than the time we spend at the things we have to do.

If you are prone to working too much, it may be as hard for you to make time for leisure activities as it is for someone with too little work incentive to work harder. If that's true, you might think of whatever you do outside of work as "productive leisure-time" activities, as James J. Sheeran refers to them in his book, *How to Skyrocket Your Income.* It will then be easier to go the next step—doing them just for the fun of it. Here are six productive leisure-time activities that Sheeran suggests:

1. Become an expert (at something).
2. Try local politics.
3. Try teaching.
4. Be an omnivorous reader.
5. Increase communicative skills.
6. Continue formal education.

Ask yourself this question: If I retired tomorrow, what would I want to do with my time? Whatever your answers are, pick a few of those choices, and start doing them now. If you are a full-time housekeeper, are you putting off doing things for yourself until the children are older? How about finding an hour or two now, even once a week, that's just for you. Hire a babysitter and go off to a museum or to a movie—for yourself.

Exercising takes time. You've got to love it, relish the competition (if applicable), or believe it's so crucial to your health and well-being that you'll make the time.

Consider some time-saving exercise suggestions:

1. Make exercise a part of your everyday routine—walk instead of taking the car, ride a bicycle on errands, do isometrics while you're on the phone, put in ten minutes of calisthenics every morning.
2. Keep your weight down so you exercise to stay fit, not principally as a weight-reducing measure.

106

3. If you absolutely hate exercising, try doing it with someone else, so it's a social as well as a physical activity: misery loves company.
4. Use the reward system discussed earlier: "If I exercise this week, I'll . . ." At some point, you may find the exercising has become its own reward.

Today—not tomorrow—decide on a realistic exercise/sports regimen, whether walking an extra two miles a day or taking a dance or karate class. Don't overload yourself by registering for exercise classes every night of the week. That kind of unrealistic overcommitment will probably result in abandoning the effort. Consider what types of exercises (sports activities) you enjoy and would like to participate in on a regular basis, perhaps combined with other sports on an alternating basis (e.g., running three times a week and playing tennis on Saturdays, or bowling once a month and ice skating every other month). Make a commitment with yourself to follow through on a regular exercise/sports regimen, even if it's only for 15 minutes a day.

If you still can't think of exercise as anything but work, or if you have disabilities that limit the type or amount of exercise you can engage in, consider spending some of your leisure time pursuing a hobby. (If you enjoy exercise, consider a hobby as another valuable leisure-time pursuit.) A hobby can be a rewarding way to spend your time, especially since it can provide the "I did it all by myself" feeling. If you don't have a hobby, think back to your early years. What did you like to do in your spare time then that you don't find time for now? Perhaps you watched the stars, burned designs in wood, or worked with mosaic tiles. Maybe you had a chemistry set or were an amateur photographer. No matter. You can learn a completely new hobby. The key is to become adept enough at your hobby so that it is something that gives you pleasure.

Hobbies are not, however, things you have to do anyway, such as cleaning or doing the laundry. Try, if possible, to pick a hobby that is unrelated to your work. Example: You are a researcher and your profession requires you to read a lot. Reading could be your hobby, but only if you read something outside of your profession, such as short stories, mysteries, novels, poetry, or popular nonfiction.

Remember: you're not engaging in this hobby so you can compete in a national contest or have a one-person showing of your work. Initially, and perhaps always, like exercise, this one's primarily for you.

Watching TV can be a worthwhile and inexpensive form of entertainment. TV can also be a time-saver—you don't have to dress and travel to experience it. In moderation, and if watched selectively, TV can be relaxing, informative, and stimulating. However, if it is your primary leisure-time activity, you will be missing out on other ways to creatively use your free time.

There always seem to be those who can do their homework, read a book, or prepare a report, all while watching television. If you are observant, you will find that either they are only watching television or only doing their homework. Their attention may shift back and forth, but most of the time the television serves as background "noise," or the book serves as facade for the television viewing.

How many hours do you spend watching TV, especially during the hours that are considered prime time (Monday through Saturday, 8 to 11 p.m. and Sunday, 7 to 11 p.m.)? Do you watch a specific program, or an LOP (least objectionable program)? Do you even know your television viewing habits? Keep a TV log for the next week to find out what hours you watch, the programs you are watching (and why), with whom you watched, and how much enjoyment you derived from your TV viewing.

Renting or purchasing a video recorder (VCR) may, interestingly, help you diminish the total number of hours you spend watching TV but increase the pleasure you derive from the few special programs you do watch. A video recorder enables you to tape a specific program and watch it when it is convenient for you. If you are away from home, for example, or doing something else, you need not stop to watch. In that way, your time is structured around your needs rather than the TV station's programming schedule. Add to this the fact that since you can freeze or stop the tape at any point, you can avoid inadvertently missing a major plot development because of other needs. Video recorder time wasters, however, include the time it will take initially to learn how to operate a VCR, to purchase blank tapes, and the few minutes it takes to program it to record as you wish.

Outside entertainment and events can be a worthwhile leisure-time activity. The possibilities are limitless, once you invest a little time in researching what your community has to offer—from amateur and professional theater, psychodrama, and puppet shows, to try-out night at the local restaurant and bowling.

Traveling is a leisure-time activity that can occupy you (and your family) delightfully for months. You can read up on the possible places you want to visit, take time to contact friends to see if they know anyone who lives there, and explore ways to make the most of your stay.

There are also travel organizations you can join, such as the Sierra Club, American Youth Hostels, and the American Adventurers Association, with year-round day, weekend, week, or longer trips for individuals, couples, and families. One-day trips from your home—with or without a club—can provide memorable leisure-time fun. Weekend overnight trips, if you keep driving time to under two hours, may be time-saving mini-vacations. Check out bed and breakfast lodging facilities within two hours of your home. It is an inexpensive, and quaint, way to spend a weekend (in contrast to an expensive and more formal hotel/motel environment).

Photography is a leisure-time hobby that is often associated with traveling. If you're going to spend the money to buy the equipment and supplies to photograph your adventures, consider taking an introductory course in photography just so you feel more confident snapping away. If you're not interested in becoming that good a photographer, you might consider relying on an instant camera with a built-in flash and automatic focusing. What you sacrifice in quality, you gain in time.

RELATIONSHIPS

Socializing/Entertaining

The reasons people fail to socialize or entertain are: lack of interest, money, people, or time. This section will deal with the last of these reasons.

Socializing, or getting together with friends or associates, takes place outside your home; entertaining is socializing inside your home—or in some other location you have chosen—for which you are responsible for supplying the food and drink or arranging for someone else to provide it. To socialize, you might make a phone call or two, and decide when, where, and what (coffee at a café, movies, dinner, bowling, etc.), but there is very little "how" to be concerned about. The advance planning for socializing is minimal, yet, unless you have a drop-in arrangement with a friend who lives in the neighborhood or a co-worker down the hall (potential time wasters, as we've seen), socializing takes some time and effort. Spur-of-the moment guests take the least amount of effort and preparation, especially if you've stockpiled suitable food and beverages. How often you socialize, and with whom, will depend not only on what value you place on that relationship, but what other commitments you have at the time.

If possible, plan to see your friends, and to develop new acquaintances, around the times that are best for you. The holidays are a time for socializing and, generally, a favored time for entertaining—but if you happen to be studying for finals, or you're in a business such as accounting, with lots of paperwork due right after the first of the year, this may not be the best time for you.

What counts is not how busy you are, or how many people you see, but whether you feel that you are making enough time for socializing. You may find that there is sufficient socializing for you during the day or just after work that *not* socializing in the evenings and on the weekends is what you want. (You may be so over-socialized that you lack enough time for yourself or for your spouse.) You may want to schedule a night alone, or a night with your spouse, even if that means you simply read a book or watch TV. Make sure you keep those appointments as surely as you would any other commitment.

Entertaining usually requires more advance planning. As veteran caterer and party-giver Florence Lowell points out in her book, *Be a Guest At Your Own Party,* entertaining is more fun when you're relaxed. Being relaxed, if you're the host or hostess, usually means planning ahead (even if that means merely picking a date, deciding whom to invite, and hiring someone to carry out your plans for you).

You can make such a big deal about entertaining that you never find the time. If you usually keep your home reasonably clean, you won't associate entertaining with "cleaning up." The more frequently you entertain, the more comfortable you'll become at doing it. When it comes to entertaining, however, Murphy's Law is in effect more than ever—it almost always takes more time, energy, and money than you thought it would. Keeping this in mind, the simpler you make your entertaining, the more likely you will be to do it again. However, you have to be careful not to offend your guests; if they believe there was no effort involved, they may feel that you don't think they matter very much.

Make a list of your closest friends and relatives. Make a second list of those business associates and casual friends or acquaintances whom you'd like to invite over. Now look ahead at the coming year. How frequently do you want to entertain? Are there times that are better for you (or your family) than others?

Look over your list of names. Figure out what forms your entertaining should take to include these varying individuals and groups. You might, for example, have a small birthday party for your father-in-law, or a huge bash for your whole office. Have one friend over for coffee and cake, perhaps in two months, and invite two couples for dinner, three months from now. If one of your goals is to enable all your guests to have a chance to interact with one another, consider entertaining up to eight persons at the same time. Larger groups will result in some of your guests leaving as unfamiliar to others as when they arrived (which is just fine in a large party situation).

Have you ever considered giving two parties back-to-back? Those you couldn't include in the first party can be served at the second, and since your hall closet is already cleaned out, why not save time and get extra mileage out of your efforts? Have you also considered serving brunch, in lieu of dinner? I usually takes less time to plan, prepare, serve, and clean up.

Networking, Support Systems, and Friendships

Although it has long been recognized that friendship is vital during the adolescent years—as children relate to peers as a way of separating from parents and siblings in preparation for the independent roles they will assume in adulthood—it is now recognized that friendship is important as early as one year of age and throughout adulthood. Furthermore, as the number of adults who postpone marriage and remain (or become) single increases, friendship (in lieu of marital ties), is necessary for emotional well-being.

The family is a type of network—indeed the primary one—but the term *networking* is generally used to refer to non-kin groups, formally or informally organized to fill a need for information, services, or friendship shared by its members or participants. Networks can be informal—as when, for example, those who attended a camp or school together maintain a network of friends who stay in touch and meet. Formal networks, such as professional or business organizations or associations, tend to be larger and more structured; members number in the hundreds or thousands, and there are annual or monthly meetings or conferences.

Support systems include nuclear family members, formal or informal networks, such as self-help groups related to a specific interest or problem, and friendships. Friendship, an intimate relationship between two or more persons unrelated by blood or legal ties, is further defined by its level of intimacy, such as "best," "close," or "casual." Although a friendship may evolve out of networks or support groups, it is distinguished from any other relationship (including marriage, parenting, or work-related relations) in that it is an optional role. It is also a relationship between equals based on a shared appreciation of each other's personality and abilities; any hint of opportunism, as even the earliest treatises on friendship by the Greek and Roman philosophers pointed out, rules out that relationship as a genuine friendship.

Friendships need time to develop and to be maintained. Certainly not as much time as you invest in a spouse, child, or parent, but if you let other commitments come between you and a friend, you may find your friend has replaced you with someone more available. A worthwhile friend is worth that time. In *Friends, For Life,* psychologist Steve Duck outlines these benefits of friendship: "a sense of belonging, emotional integration and stability, opportunities for communication about ourselves, provision of assistance and physical support, reassurance of our worth and value, opportunity to help others, and personality support." One cautionary note: My own research, and the studies done by other social scientists, have found that it is to family that most turn for money or help when sick. If you want to maintain your friendships, you might consider that since it is an optional role, there are limitations on it. Friendship, however, provides benefits that may be lacking in a family. As one 37-year-old single woman told me: "Your family accepts you with all your faults and they love you anyway, but it's not like that with your friends." She was alluding to the fact that your friends choose you. To reinforce their choice of you (and your choice of them) you will need time together, as well as the ability to be open (self-disclosure) and to be vulnerable (able to withstand the possible end of the friendship).

Making Time for Partners and Children

Ironically it can be easier to find time for friends than for mates and children. In an intimate setting, physical presence need not mean that you're giving time. (You could be going your separate ways even under the same roof.) Friendship, since you're generally separated, requires time and effort if contact is to be maintained, whether by phone, letter, or in person. It is usually necessary to make an appointment for meeting, even if it only means calling a few minutes in advance to say "Can I come over?" Because contact is generally less frequent than with family members, and because the relationship is less intimate, different rules apply. Friends may give each other more attention when they do get together than family members ever get, because the family is around all the time. Furthermore, your expectations are lower from a friendship than from a primary intimate relationship. It may be enough for friends to get together once a month to play tennis; few marriages would tolerate that dearth of interaction.

If you feel you don't have enough time with your spouse, perhaps some of the following suggestions will be useful:

1. Realize that perfect relationships exist only between perfect people.
2. If possible, spend some time together during the workday, perhaps meeting for lunch on occasion, so you're not just an "after five" couple.
3. Don't wait for your annual vacation to get away; plan mini-getaway weekends together to break up your routine.
4. If you feel a need to get away alone now and then, do it. It doesn't necessarily mean there's something wrong with your relationship; a little absence does make the heart grow fonder.
5. How much do you really know about what your partner does? Take the time to read books, take courses, and talk to others in that line of work (and vice versa) so you can better understand each other's daily experiences and routines.
6. Have a leisure-time activity that you regularly do together.
7. Share parenting and household responsibilities by working them out in a way that's best for both of you.

What about sexual intimacy? Once again, personal preferences as to frequency, duration, style, and enjoyment are paramount, but if sex is important to you and your partner, make the time for it, no matter how busy you are. Although sexual intimacy is associated with marital bliss, some, such as Herbert G. Zerof in *Finding Intimacy,* say it is being overemphasized today. If you are giving sex the proper emphasis in your relationship, however, but are failing to find time for it, sex therapist Avodah Offit, in *Night Thoughts,* suggests making the time. Offit advises couples, on a regular basis, to set aside time exclusively devoted to their intimate relationship. If you wait to be spontaneous, it may never happen.

Consider the quality, and quantity, of time you spend with your children. How much time do you give to them? "It's important to spend time with your children because they need to know they're loved and cared about," says Linda, 31, a full-time college student who is also the mother of three children, ages 13, 11, and 4. "If you don't spend time with them, they won't feel that they're wanted, loved, or needed. They have to be taught. It takes time to teach them the proper things—values, morals, and all those things," Linda adds.

You might also ask yourself how much time your children give *you.* After all, the awareness that loving is a two-way commitment starts in the home. If children think that they are entitled to love, and need not give any back, problems with intimacy can emerge in their adult years. Jim, 18, a freshman in college still living at home, finds time for his parents during the week and on weekends. "During the week I spend time with them at dinner and at night I hang around and talk and watch TV with them. On the weekends, we go out to dinner together. In the summer, we play a lot of tennis together and golf or go to the movies. I try to balance it out with my parents and my friends." Patricia, 24, working full-time as an administrative assistant and still living at home, does not spend much time with her parents. Patricia explains: "I'm selfish and I'd spend time with my parents but I don't have time for it. My time goes to friends and to personal things. We're supposed to have meals together but my mother works at night. I stopped spending time with my parents when I started going to college because then it's okay to socialize, 'Let's go out.' "

If you think your children fail to give you enough time, consider if they are reflecting patterns from your own childhood, as well as how much time you currently give your *own* parents.

Consider, however, that no matter how much time you give to those you love—or they give to you—the time spent may fall short of your expectations. That might be a reflection of how you spend your time together—and what you do—rather than who you spend it with. Think about doing something new and exciting together.

You might also consider that all of us need time alone in addition to time together. If one partner is around people all day, and the other is not, they may have opposite needs during non-work time. (Similarly, children want their parents' attention and the parent may not have any attention to give just then.) Management consultant Gisele Richardson has noted that people need three types of time for emotional health: diffused time (exposure to people); qualitative time (one-to-one intimate contact); and alone-time (private moments to digest the stimuli from the other two types of time). If your spouse, child, parent, or friend needs "alone time," don't take it as rejection and stew in an unproductive way. Use the time you would have spent with them to your best advantage; you'll be able to appreciate the time together even more.

Perhaps you would spend more time with your spouse, children, or parents if you could just "communicate." In the next section, we'll look at ways of bettering family communication.

Improving Communication at Home

Good communication in intimate situations can be tremendously rewarding, but it takes time, and even then it is sometimes difficult or impossible to achieve. Why? According to family communication experts Miller, Wackman, and Nunnally, co-authors of *Straight Talk,* four fears get in the way of effective communication: fears of speaking out, of fighting, of intimacy, and of commitment.

Communication problems present at the beginning of a romantic relationship may be ignored because the need to connect deeply with someone, and the newness of the relationship, carry a couple along. In a desire to win each other over, differences may be minimized. "He'll change," "I'll get used to that," "She'll get to understand what I mean" allow a couple to move from acquaintanceship to intimacy.

A faulty belief hampering couple communication is that the couple is the sum of the two individuals. A couple, however, is a third entity, with a life of its own, based on the interactions of the two units. Sally plus George is as unique a unit as Sally and George are as individuals.

Communication at home may be improved if both partners take the time to understand, and change, the verbal and nonverbal cues that they give each other, and if they work to improve their listening skills and their ability to give feedback. We communicate with two languages, one verbal and one nonverbal. Just as the meaning of time, and language, varies from culture to culture, and within a culture, so too nonverbal cues may have varying meanings. For example, in *The Hidden Dimension,* Edward T. Hall points out that in Arab cultures a potential wife may be rejected by those arranging the marriage if she "does not smell nice."

How many of the following nonverbal cues do you pay attention to, in yourself and in your partner?

facial expressions
eye contact
voice tone and quality
gross oral expressions or sounds (sighs, clearing the throat, laughing, crying)
match of nonverbal and verbal cues ("I love you" said with a sneer)
gestures
posture (body stance)

distance (How close or far away from each other do you stand, sit, sleep?)

physical appearance (What messages are being communicated by dress or clothing, hair style, or make-up?)

demeanor

silence

body mirroring (If bodies are linked up with each other, or if breathing is matched, it is said to be an indication of rapport)

George and Mary do not have body mirroring. George noticed this when he and Mary walked a few blocks to the movie theater. George became angry that Mary was always six steps behind him. Unwittingly, Mary was demonstrating how out-of-step she felt with George. Experts suggest that when walking and breathing are in harmony, communication is optimal. Do George and Mary throw in the towel because they are out of sync, or can they improve their communication (and hence their relationship)?

Social scientist Joseph M. Strayhorn, Jr., author of *Talking It Out*, states that "conflict is the rule, not the exception, in human relationships." Strayhorn, and other experts on interpersonal communication, believe that, with practice, a couple can improve how they communicate. Strayhorn divides the messages that a couple give each other into two types: facilitative (rewarding) and obstructive (inhibiting). To improve communication, facilitative statements should replace obstructive ones. For example, "You should buy me flowers" is an obstructive "You should" message. This type of statement implies that the speaker is an authority, or parent figure, sitting in judgment of what is right and wrong. "I like to receive flowers" is a facilitative statement; it places the responsibility on the speaker to decide and state her likes and dislikes, and on the listener to decide to use or ignore the information. A couple determined to improve their communication should consider studying Strayhorn's detailed *Talking It Out*. The book illustrates how to substitute facilitative for obstructive statements so that couple communication is more rewarding.

Of course not all couples experience communication problems; some may be more adept at communicating or at handling conflict. Unfortunately it may take arguments or threatened or actual separation to motivate better communication. With time (Dorothy Tennov suggests in *Love and Limerance* that it will take three years) just the initial chemistry you felt may be insufficient to sustain a complex living-together relationship.

Before the first child arrives, a couple may divide their time among work, personal, and professional pursuits as well as competing relationships. It is easier for a couple to tell another adult that they are busy (and need time for each other) than it will be to tell a child (especially during the formative years). Thus all couples experience dramatic changes upon the birth of their first child. A dyadic romantic relationship becomes a triad, for starters. The new triad is easier to maintain, because the third member helps to perpetuate the group, but it is a less intimate group than the former twosome; couple communication may be put on the back burner. Although the couple now have someone in common to talk about, communication unrelated to their parenting roles may take a turn for the worse. As the family grows in number, the interactions may become less satisfying and more complicated. Either or both partners may not even like being a parent—it's not something one can really know in advance.

According to sociologist Janet Mancini Billson, a professor at Rhode Island College and an expert on small groups, all small groups, including the nuclear family (marital couple + children) have to deal with issues that revolve around "SIP" (*S*tructure, *I*ntimacy, and *P*articipation). Structure refers to everything from what subjects are discussed over dinner to when dinner will take place, where, and on which dishes (formal or informal). Intimacy takes into account each family member's basic capacity for closeness, as well as shifts in intimacy needs and abilities. Participation encompasses how much involvement primary group members will have. Let's take a participation issue that might emerge for a dating couple. Will they see each other a few nights a week, or every night? If they marry, upon the birth of the first child, will the husband be actively involved in childrearing, or will those responsibilities fall mainly on the wife?

Conflicting needs of each group member, highlighted by SIP, emerged in interviews I conducted with a working mother and her daughter. The mother, a public relations director for a perfume company, emphasized how close she is to her daughter; her twelve-year-old daughter said she only talks to her mother when they go horseback riding once a week. Weekday nights, she and her sister eat alone; her parents eat dinner much later, in their master bedroom. This family seems to have conflicts in all SIP areas.

How might you use SIP to improve communication in your home setting? First, upon reflection or with the aid of outside advisers or observers (therapists, religious leaders, close friends), try to determine how accurately you are reading your home situation, and how much distortion is caused by your own unmet needs and expectations. It may be that the communication problems are only temporary; your spouse is "under the gun" at work and he wants to be left alone most weekday nights. For a few months after Carl's father died, Carl became withdrawn and could not be intimate with his wife. Judy's new job demands so much structure—arriving at a certain time, only an hour for lunch, strict adherence to deadlines—that Judy wants her free time to be unstructured and unplanned.

Use SIP to improve communication by using feedback, the way to tell someone how his or her behavior affects you. It differs from amateur psychologizing about *why* someone is acting in a certain way by focusing on *what* you observe (verbally and nonverbally). It gives your partner the opportunity to learn from the feedback, while still maintaining control over why he does things or how he will change.

In order for feedback to be helpful, it should be given in a nonjudgmental way. (Feedback can also stress what is positive.) For example, instead of telling someone that you think he is a loudmouth, consider saying, "I would like to have a chance to do more talking when we get together." Instead of telling someone that she dresses badly you might say, "That blouse clashes with your skirt."

For feedback to be most effective, it should occur soon after the behavior in question. Feedback should also be given out of concern and caring, not as a form of hostility and bullying. Clinical sociologist John Glass shares these additional suggestions for giving, and receiving, feedback:

- Focus feedback on the sharing of ideas and information rather than on giving advice
- Focus feedback on the value it may have to the recipient, and not on the value or "release" that it provides the person giving the feedback
- Focus feedback on *what* is said rather than *why* it is said
- Focus feedback on the behavior rather than the person

In addition to the suggestions thus far in this section, review the tips for improving communication at work that were noted in Chapter Four. Why it is important to make more time for your important family members is a question that almost everyone can answer; how to make that time, however, seems less within our reach. Some suggestions earlier in this chapter for including some time during your workday for your spouse should be reviewed. Children, especially if both parents are working, need to have some time with you before their bedtime. Sharing meals is one way of ensuring collective time together. If weekday evenings are impossible to schedule, be sure one or more weekend meals are shared. Although time together should be an ongoing aspect of your home life, have scheduled family activities or at least family vacations or days or weekends away together once or twice a year. Time for family members should not end with departure from home. Grown children and your own parents need your time, since ties have to be continually strengthened, and new information about each other shared.

As the next chapter further demonstrates, the kind of work you do—whether you are a nine-to-five or self-employed worker, a homemaker, or a student—will generate time demands unique to that role. As your roles shift, so too should the way you creatively manage your time.

TERMS

prime time
VCR
facilitative communication
SIP
diffused time
LOP

body mirroring
obstructive communication
feedback
alone time
qualitative time

REFERENCES

BARKAS, J.L. "Friendship Throughout Life." New York: Public Affairs Committee, 1983.

――――. *The Help Book.* New York: Charles Scribner's Sons, 1979. An annotated directory to getting help in fifty-two areas of concern including counseling, employment, mental health, and suicide prevention.

BERLAND, THEODORE. *The Fitness Fact Book: The Complete Guide to Diet, Exercise and Sport.* New York: New American Library, 1981. A concise guide to the benefits of exercise, rating your fitness, treating aches and pains, and how to relax.

DAVIS, MURRAY S. *Intimate Relations.* New York: Free Press, 1973. An in-depth study of intimacy, from meeting through coupling.

DIAGRAM GROUP. *The Complete Encyclopedia of Exercises.* New York: Van Nostrand Reinhold Company, 1981.

DUCK, STEVE. *Friends, For Life: The Psychology of Close Relationships.* Brighton, England: Harvester Press, 1983.

GOTTMAN, JOHN, CLIFF NOTARIUS, JONNI GONSO, and HOWARD MARKMAN. *A Couple's Guide to Communication.* Champaign, Ill.: Research Press, 1976. A step-by-step guide to achieving "good communication," which the authors explain means "having the impact you intended to have."

HALL, EDWARD T. *The Hidden Dimension.* Garden City, N.Y.: Doubleday & Company, Inc., 1966.

KRIEGER, DOLORES. *The Therapeutic Touch: How to Use Your Hands to Help or to Heal.* Englewood Cliffs, N.J.: Prentice-Hall, Inc., 1979.

KUNTZLEMAN, CHARLES T. *The Complete Book of Walking.* Skokie, Ill.: Publications International Ltd., 1979. Walking can be an effective tool for weight loss or maintenance, release of emotional tension, and physical fitness.

LANDERS, ANN. "Parents: What Do You Owe Your Children?" *Family Circle,* November 15, 1977, pp. 2, 152–53.

LIPNACK, JESSICA, and JEFFREY STAMPS. *Networking.* Garden City, N.Y.: Dolphin Book/Doubleday & Company, Inc., 1982.

LOWELL, FLORENCE, and NORMA LEE BROWNING. *Be a Guest At Your Own Party.* New York: M. Evans Company, Inc., 1980. Tips and recipes for entertaining.

MILLER, SHEROD, DANIEL WACKMAN, ELAM NUNNALLY, and CAROL SALINE. *Straight Talk.* New York: New American Library, 1982.

OFFIT, AVODAH K., M.D. *Night Thoughts: Reflections of a Sex Therapist.* New York: Congdon & Lattes, Inc., 1981.

RICHARDSON, GISELE. "Learn to Structure Personal Time Needs," *Botton Line Personal,* July 15, 1980, pp. 9–10.

ROHRLICH, JAY B., M.D. *Work and Love: The Crucial Balance.* New York: Summit Books, Simon & Schuster, 1980.

RUBIN, ZICK. *Children's Friendships.* Cambridge, Mass.: Harvard University Press, 1980.

SHEERAN, JAMES J. *How to Skyrocket Your Income.* New York: Frederick Fell Publishers, Inc., 1976.

STRAYHORN, JOSEPH M., JR. *Talking It Out: A Guide to Effective Communication and Problem Solving.* Champaign, Ill.: Research Press, 1977.

TENNOV, DOROTHY. *Love and Limerance: The Experience of Being in Love.* New York: Stein and Day, 1979.

ZEROF, HERBERT G. *Finding Intimacy.* Minneapolis, Minn.: Winston Press, Inc., 1978.

EXERCISES

1. If you do not already have an established exercise regimen, plan one that you will realistically carry out. If you work, just after work and before coming home once a week might be a practical time for exercise. If you don't work, or are in school, pick a "slow day," perhaps a Friday, when you have more time or incentive.

2. Pick a time for getting together with your friends that is convenient for you. Consider all the various commitments in your life and plan a party you will give six months to a year in the future.

3. Decide when and how you will allot time regularly to actively communicating (including listening) with each important person in your life, e.g., spouse, child, best friend.

4. Make a chart of all your free time. Are there blocks of time, or just minutes here and there? What activities, people, things are you now filling up this time with? Is there anything you'd like to do differently? Create an ideal free time schedule that you'd like to strive toward.

5. Do you have one or more hobbies? If you don't, start thinking about what you'd like to do in your free time, and set a target date for actually beginning your hobby.

7
How Time
Management Works

Time is the most valuable thing a man can spend.

THEOPHRASTUS
(?–278 B.C.)

STRUCTURING TIME

Changing circumstances dictate altering how you manage your time. Your primary work role may be that of executive, but your family relations and community activities are other roles that demand your time. You may be an accountant, paid by the hour, with numerous outside obligations, or a self-employed researcher, paid by the project, who is active in sports and cultural activities. Few of us play only one role; how best to perform each role is a prevailing theme when planning your time.

The sections that follow deal with structuring time for various roles: nine-to-fivers, self-employed, students, or homemakers. You may want to read each section, however, since you may benefit from applying time management techniques more typical of another role to your own.

For Nine-to-fivers and Other Workers

Few are exactly "nine-to-fivers," since "start-up" time—getting dressed, having breakfast, commuting back and forth—can aid or interfere with actual work time as much as how early you get to the office, how late you stay, and how much "after hours" studying, entertaining, or traveling you are expected to do.

All of the tips given in Chapter Three for being organized and in Chapter Four for enhancing your time at work apply particularly to those in structured work situations. Those in formal settings may benefit even more from stringent self-checks, since much work may be so routinized one could mistakenly believe that providing one's physical presence is equivalent to working. Your boss may tell you to do a report, and then ask you to do six other things. You let the report slide, complete the other things, and when she asks for that report, you say you need a little more time "to polish it," and then write it in a hurry. A professional might be so involved with handling her clients that she does not invest enough time in increasing her client load; her practice may not grow as quickly as it could. She may fail to keep up with her professional education if no one tells her—or makes her—do it.

If you work in a structured setting, try to pinpoint the uninterrupted work periods available to you, e.g., from arrival to lunch or from after lunch till departure. Then, except for necessary interruptions, use those blocks of work time to concentrate and accomplish your short- and long-term goals. Try to reserve fifteen minutes at the end of each day to review that day's "to do" list, noting where you achieved your goals, where you fell short, and setting your priorities for the next day. As we've seen, it may be counter-productive to your job, or to your personal needs, to frequently need to work outside your office. Trains, chaotic family rooms, and rooms where dinner parties are in progress are not the most conducive places to work efficiently. Good planning should minimize the frequency with which this occurs; remember, unrealistic deadlines should be revised well in advance of any due dates.

In years to come, more and more firms may be using the computer to devise plans to increase corporate efficiency. Weiner and Company, a certified public accounting firm based in Manhattan, is one firm that has already done just that, and with excellent results, according to its president, Ron Weiner. The time management system Weiner devised is called "PROPLAN" (PROfessional PROductivity PLANning), and it has been in effect since 1981. Weiner found that as his firm grew from twelve employees, in 1976, to its current size of about eighty persons, inefficiencies increased as well. Accountants sell their skills, but Weiner found it easier to devise a time management program based on billable hours, a more quantifiable measure. At Weiner's firm, which includes office personnel, juniors, semi-juniors, seniors, supervisors, managers, and partners, all hours are not equal since an employee's skills level and, consequently, the cost to the client for that hour, will differ. Weiner and Company wanted to figure out how a client could get the job done as efficiently, competently, and inexpensively as possible. Before PROPLAN, an audit that might take a week would be completed, but the way it was accomplished was like Pareto's rule: 80 percent of the work got done in the last 20 percent of the time.

With PROPLAN, the computer print-out allows for more planning, and the execution of the plan is spelled out in steps, each step lasting about half a day (three hours). PROPLAN enables Weiner and Company to give more accurate, and economical, time and cost estimates to prospective clients. The computer print-out provides a road map for the audit; skill levels, not individuals, are indicated. Specific job assignments are made by office personnel, not by partners, as had been the procedure. Weiner's PROPLAN uses basic time management principles that you can apply in your own work situation, such as: breaking projects or weeks into three-hour time periods, each with a specific task; delegating tasks that are below or above your skills level; setting a realistic limit on the hours you work; and being more effective within those limits.

For the Self-Employed

Although being self-employed carries the connotation of working "for yourself," virtually all self-employed workers are dependent upon clients, patients, patrons, and similar fee-generating income sources. Sometimes being self-employed can place greater restrictions on freedom than working for a single employer (whether another individual or a huge conglomerate). For many self-employed persons, obtaining work can involve as much time and effort as doing it. By contrast, the traditional nine-to-fiver, by the very nature of the work structure, has work "handed to him."

If you are self-employed, you should rate yourself as an employer. Do you have a pension plan, vacation time, sick days, time for personal leave, maternity leave? If someone else employed you, you'd certainly expect some of those benefits. Don't drive yourself into an unpensioned grave for the seeming luxury of self-employment; you might turn out to be the worst employer you've ever had. Self-employment can mean increased freedom in your daily affairs; it can also mean increased pressure, fewer hours with your friends and family, and little financial security. It may be harder for you to find the time to perform your skill, or create your product, if you are unable to delegate the busywork that would fall on someone else's shoulders if you were in a corporate environment with extensive support services.

Creative and effective time management may make or break a self-employed person. Bob, 53, a self-employed counselor, says, "I feel more pressure because I know that the temptation to just sit down and watch TV or to lie in bed till ten o'clock in the morning is very great and there's no one there to say, 'Hey, get up and punch a time clock.'"

Adhering to a fixed schedule, with provisions for overtime, seems to be the time management technique of choice for those who are self-employed in creative professions. Jack, 67, a successful self-employed nonfiction writer for over 40 years, writes: "The *only* way to become successful at free-lancing is to run your operation like a business. . . . Hit your desk at specific hours. Otherwise the tendency to goof off will take over. . . . Be prepared, too, for overtime work. There will be times when deadlines must be met, and hence night work and weekend work will be necessary."

Factors that affect time management for the self-employed are: where you work (in your home or "outside"); the pattern of work (at a desk or traveling most of the time); and the nature of work (whether a skill or a product). A psychotherapist with an outside office and a secretary, for example, may sit in a room most of the day with patients coming to see her. The therapist will have a structure imposed on her by the presence, and schedule, of her secretary and clients. It will be more difficult for her to "goof off" than it might be for a self-employed artist who works alone at home. An actor who earns his living making TV commercials may spend eight hours "out on call," with four of those hours spent "waiting" for appointments, or between auditions. He may have to be more disciplined during periods when there are no auditions or parts to be had since he probably does not have an outside "office."

Self-employed persons who work at home create solutions to the "how to get going in the morning when you don't commute to work" situation. Brian, 59, a self-employed labor mediator who works at home, begins his day by walking his dog, buying the newspaper, and reading it over breakfast. Unless he has an outside appointment, he begins each workday by nine, as if he just arrived at corporate headquarters.

A factor for those who are self-employed to consider is a phenomenon that I call *time lag*. Let's say that right now you've got more work than you can handle. You might feel your problem is not having enough time to do all the work that's coming your way. Think again. "I was right at the end of finishing a book I had worked on for the past two years when a big newspaper called me," said Arlene, a woman in her forties who writes articles and books. "The editor needed an article, and I said I couldn't do it because I was finishing my book. I told her I'd give her a call when I was free." A few months later, when Arlene was free, she called, but the editor wouldn't take her call. Now Arlene had the time, but couldn't find editors who wanted her time—a classic example of time lag.

The reason that the self-employed have the problem of time lag is difficulty in looking past what they are currently doing, and planning ahead so that something is "in the pipeline," and ready to be started when the current work is completed. The worst time to get work—whether it's a job or a new assignment—is when you're not working. Those who are self-employed have to force themselves to devise basic time management principles to fit their specific needs, i.e. x, y, and z (future objectives) must be pursued while a and b (current objectives) are ongoing.

Avoiding time lag if you are self-employed requires sharp judgment as to how long a given project will actually take—not how long you'd like it to take. That way you can give yourself or your client a realistic deadline (starting *and* ending) for the next project, whether for two weeks or two years.

You might find it useful to create an organized system for keeping track of your assignments, as well as any potential projects that you are currently circulating or proposing. Try using the "A B C" approach. Using cards or notebooks, apply the "who, what, where, when, how, why" analysis. Here's one example of the kind of system you might devise:

Sample Card for Keeping Track of Assignments

Project Description: _____

Client: _____

Date Assigned: _____

Due Date: _____

Actual Submission Date: _____

Length/Type: _____

Fee: _____

Budget: _____

Expenses: _____

Outcome: _____

For Students*

Let's look at the basics of time management in a school situation, remembering that the time pressures on someone returning to school later in life differ from those facing the younger student. Too, the student with a part-time or full-time job will conduct himself differently from one who doesn't work.

Each school year comes predefined as a block of time with certain objectives. Unlike a year-in, year-out job, school is easily divisible into distinct periods with formal beginnings, well defined endings, and structured checkpoints along the way. Take advantage of those clear divisions; they make managing your time as a student somewhat easier.

Have an academic planning calendar that matches your schedule for the forthcoming year, and enter all course requirements (assignments, paper due dates, exams) that you know are due in the coming semester or school year onto your master calendar. Now, allocate certain blocks of time based on these commitments. For example, you might wish to reserve the week before midterms for studying so that you will not unnecessarily distract yourself with

*For time management tips for teachers, see Appendix VII.

other commitments. You might also want to block out the week after final examinations for social and fun activities (and those inescapable duties you've put off while studying).

Some students find the "short shift" system of studying to be most effective. As one third-year law student put it: "I usually work in short shifts, of no longer than an hour, and I give myself incentives to push myself. Like I tell myself if I get through *x* amount of work to do in the next hour, then I'll go play basketball for an hour." He's also a crammer, doing a lot of reading on his own, playing sports, and going out with his friends the rest of the time. "Right before finals, for a week or two, I do all the things I've been putting off all semester—most of my reading and studying."

A young woman, now 21, in her junior year of college in Oklahoma, and majoring in business administration, did not find cramming before exams worked for her. Her grades suffered so much because she went to football games rather than studying, that she dropped out of school for two years, and returned home to Florida to work for her father. Two years later, she returned to school, with a renewed commitment to apply herself.

Whether you study in short shifts or in long stretches, whether you study every night or cram right before exams, whether you retain what you learn only until the exam is over, or for the rest of your life, remembering and learning are the keys to success as a student—not how many hours you put in. In their book, *Study Smarts,* co-authors Kesselman-Turkel and Peterson, free-lance writers and teachers at the University of Wisconsin at Madison, provide a summary of Dr. Walter Pauk's OK4R system, one of the many systems devised to help in remembering what you read. (OK4R is an acronym for *Overview, Key ideas, Read, Rite, Relate,* and *Review.*)

To save time, learn speedreading and speedwriting.

You might find it helpful to have an orderly system for taking notes on what you're reading. The card on page 129 is a sample of one that could be adapted to your needs. (This particular one would be useful in doing a research paper, or familiarizing yourself with the literature on a given topic.)

You will also need a place that is conducive to study—as quiet and free of distractions as possible. Some find library cubicles quiet; others can only study alone in an empty room. No one solution will work for everyone; a library may be best for some students, and a time waster for others (who can only study at the kitchen table).

Similarly, you might find, in spite of the costs involved, that purchasing books, when appropriate, saves you time that might be spent searching in the library (only to discover that one copy is "out" and the second copy has fifty pages torn out.) Libraries can be marvelous research tools—for out-of-print books, expensive references or directories, and back issues of magazines and journals. For very new materials, however, especially paperback books, you

Bibliographic Information	Library call No. _____
Author(s): Title: Place of Publication: Publisher: Year of publication:	
Summary:	
Why This Work Is Important:	
Compared to Other Works:	
Criticism:	
1st reading: _____ 2nd reading: _____ 3rd reading: _____	

may be better off acquiring these books because: (a) you'll want them for your personal library; (b) they're so new the library hasn't received them yet; or (c) you'll want them for longer than the borrowing period allows. However, don't fall into the trap of buying books, or photocopying articles or specific pages, that remain unread.

Now let's look at the time demands on the older student. Taking an occasional course in an adult education program, whether learning about "The Novels of James Joyce" or "Basic Photography," is one form of continuing or career education; it is relatively inexpensive and not very time-consuming. A commitment to a full-time degree program requires more of a juggling act—job, school, family, and friends—requiring sacrifices from everyone involved (but primarily from the student). At first, everyone may be sympathetic when studies preclude Thanksgiving this year at Cousin Rose's in Pennsylvania, but when you can't get away next year, or the following year, Cousin Rose may be distinctly less understanding. One who takes on this additional educational commitment has set his priorities and acted on them. He is willing to endure the negatives for what he perceives as an overall positive result.

Whether you are a typical young student or an older one, poor time management during the school term may contribute to test anxiety. Joe Molnar, a psychotherapist who runs workshops for overcoming test anxiety, says: "Not being adequately prepared, a cause of test anxiety, may be the consequence of procrastination about studying throughout the semester.

Behind procrastination and poor time habits can be fears of success and failure. Procrastination is simply a way of dealing with those conflicts."

Another time management consideration unique to students is that most often the student years are a high-gear, short-lived period that generally warps all notion of time. Students, especially those who work while attending school, may drive themselves at an inhuman pace for several years. Pockets of time previously spent relaxing or socializing are suddenly put to maximum and intense use. Upon finishing school, however, it may be unrealistic and unhealthy to attempt to perpetuate those high-gear time schedules. Similarly, the other extreme—becoming lazy and without any drive as a reaction to those intense years—is just as ill-advised. Thus, while in the student role, if at all possible, pace yourself and include some socializing and relaxing. In that way, the months or years in school will have served as a training ground for creative time management in high-pressure situations.

For Homemakers

A magazine editor's husband stays at home and takes care of their two children while she's at the office. A woman with four children under the age of four, whose husband's salary is not enough, wants to take a job to earn some extra money and "just to get out of the house" a few hours a week. Two executives marry, have twins, and both continue working full time; they have day care help and a cleaning lady. These are just a few examples of the multiplicity of situations, and choices, open to adults, single or coupled, with or without children. A woman's decision to work after marrying or becoming a parent is viewed today as a personal and economic decision; there are fewer rules than twenty-five years ago. Each woman, and couple, decides what's best; those decisions affect how they will spend their time. Time management will be affected by work arrangements, how many children are present, their ages, how much cleaning or child-care help is available, and, in households of two or more, the division of labor agreed upon by the couple.

The theme that ran throughout my interviews with homemakers, whether or not they had other jobs, was that parenting obligations are their biggest time demand. (Those who stay home with young children, and do not work, chose to be with their children and temporarily traded their own careers and additional income for full-time parenting responsibilities.) Few now view the non-parenting years as stressful in terms of time. Jessica, 32, a full-time homemaker living in a Connecticut suburb, has two children, ages four and six, and is married to a lawyer. In comparing the years of her marriage before and after her children were born, Jessica says: "There was always time then. There's never enough time now." Marie, 31, a full-time homemaker in Queens, New York, is married to a schoolteacher and the mother of a two-year-old daughter. When her daughter was born, Marie quit her lucrative full-time job as production coordinator for a printer. "My husband and I refer to those early years of our marriage as the single years—married before kids," Marie says. Sara, 31, a corporate executive, married and the mother of a two-year-old, works full time, has full-time help at home, and prefers being at the office as much as any other nine-to-fiver. Sara says: "When I got married I told my husband, 'I don't like cleaning or cooking and I'm always going to work.'" And she has.

"I loved the job," Marie, who was earning over $40,000 a year, says, "but it was very high-powered and it became a bit much." For now, Marie wants to handle all the child-care responsibilities herself. Marie's cleaning chores are the same as before; she kept the cleaning lady that she used when she was working. Child-care demands structure her day but her husband, a school teacher, is home by three-thirty, so her days are "short." The only chore Marie would like help with is cooking. "If tomorrow I wake up and I feel unhappy being home, I'll go back to work," Marie concludes, adding that I may have interviewed her on a "good day."

As noted in Chapter Five, housekeeping chores are the least desirable aspect of homemaking reported by Oakley's study of London housewives. Hired help may not be feasible for economic reasons; even with help, there are still chores a homemaker may have to attend to. Jessica, the Connecticut housewife with two children, spends 5½ hours each day in household chores. Jessica explains: "Two hours for dinner. An hour a day for laundry. It takes me an hour to do [clean] the whole upstairs. Half an hour for breakfast and half an hour for lunch. Half an hour to pick them up at school. But I don't think of it that way because it's something I go along and do. And I don't keep a spotless house."

Parenting responsibilities, even if a parent works and has full-time help, consume the evenings and weekends. Jessica suggests spending as much time with your children as you enjoy, not more because you "should." "I like kids," Jessica says. "I can spend twenty-four hours a day, seven days a week with kids. Usually I need a break from kids once every three or four months. But it's important that if you don't want to spend a lot of time with your kids, you shouldn't do it, or feel guilty about it. If you're happier working, you're going to have a much better relationship with your children, husband, friends [if you work]."

Corporations are recognizing that parenting presents time demands that may create stress for employees of either sex. In response to those pulls, companies are now sponsoring seminars during the workday to help employed parents cope better. A direct reaction to those seminars has been the formation of informal networks of parents within corporations who offer each other support about their mutual time problems.

Women who are full-time homemakers have time problems of a different sort from homemakers who also have outside jobs. Jessica explains:

"Women who work don't have all the extracurricular things that the mothers who stay home have to do. They don't have to be the room mothers. They don't have to be the chauffeurs. They don't have to be the ones who get the calls when the kids in the neighborhood are sick. They don't have to allot time for certain things and they set their priorities differently."

Pam Young and Peggy Jones, sisters and mothers who were then full-time homemakers, lifted themselves "out of the pigpen"—and wrote a bestseller about their program, *Sidetracked Home Executives*. They changed their lives by establishing and adhering to a time management system with just a few basic rules, such as:

1. Wake up half an hour earlier than the rest of the family and get dressed.
2. Make the bed before doing any other chores.
3. Stop watching soap operas on TV.
4. Spend one weekday doing what you want to do (free of chores and errands).

Young and Jones also devised a system of 3 x 5 cards to organize their household chores. By applying time management principles to household tasks they were able to create order in their homes and find time for their own interests.

"Time for myself" was a theme that homemakers with or without children, with or without outside jobs, stressed in our interviews. Whether it's working out at the gym, taking long walks alone, writing a novel while the baby is napping, or taking up yoga while the children are small (and teaching it at a university once they are older), having personal and professional goals of one's own is important. Jessica explains: "I've always taken a day for myself. When my kids were little, one day a week I had a sitter. Now they're both in school so I don't find I [usually] need any more time than that. [But] if I need more time for myself, I'll get up at five in the morning, instead of seven, or I'll go to bed later."

Gloria, who has four children under four, wishes she used the time when her children are napping or asleep, or her husband is at work, in a more productive way. "But you get caught in the middle of 'Well now I can sit and relax and read the newspaper,' so I end up wasting time, which is really terrible, because I would rather be doing something creative. I waste about four or five hours a day." San Francisco time management expert Donna Goldfein has advice for homemakers who waste too much time reading the newspaper:

> One of my clients said it best: "The clue I give myself that I'm procrastinating is when I get to the classified ads and I'm still reading." I think the habit of reading the paper [especially] in the morning is because the woman is past making lunches . . . and she thinks, "Now it's my time." I don't think the reading of the paper gives her anything more than a procrastinated hour and

sometimes longer. The news can be equally as understood by turning on the TV news while doing other things. The newspaper can be a trap of moving time along in the morning but not moving yourself along.

The telephone can be another trap for the full-time homemaker. If friends and family know she is at home, they may call and want to have extended conversations, discussions they would probably never feel comfortable engaging in if she were working in an office. Homemakers need to master the art of dealing with telephone interruptions. (Review the sections on telephone interruptions in Chapter Four.)

An alternative to a full-time job for homemakers, especially those with small children, is part-time work inside or outside the home. *Women Working Home* by Marion Behr and Wendy Lazar (New Jersey-WWH Press, 1981) and *A Part-Time Career for a Full-Time You* by JoAnne Alter (Boston: Houghton Mifflin, 1982) are two resources for homemakers who are considering part-time work. The increase in women working part-time outside the home has been notable: between 1970 and 1978, the increase was 36 percent (from 874,000 to 1,185,000) for women in professional and technical jobs and 59 percent (from 164,000 to 261,000) for women in managerial and administrative jobs. Part-time or full-time work inside the home includes traditional telephone sales work as well as self-employment in service and creative fields such as consulting, typing, writing, the arts, and so on. Homemakers interested in these home-based working options should consult resources on working at home, such as *Worksteads* by Jeremy Joan Hewes (Garden City, New York: Dolphin Books, 1981), as well as the Association of Part-Time Professionals, based in Alexandria, Virginia, or Catalyst, based in Manhattan.

The options today for homemakers with or without children to spend their time are exciting. Ironically, it is men, who want to play a more active role in parenting, who are experiencing the conflicts between work versus family time that women have always had to face. Don, 32, a research scientist, describing how the first few months after his son's birth adversely effected his work, says: "I found I wasn't going to the lab that much. When I did, I wasn't concentrating. I just wanted to be with my son. To watch him sleeping. To bathe him and feed him. I'm forcing myself to get back into my work now. I have to."

MAKING PRODUCTIVE USE OF YOUR "HIDDEN" TIME

"Hidden" time is time that you previously wasted or consumed with distractions that you turn into productive time for pursuing your priority tasks. What are your "hidden" times? Think about your average workday, weekday evening, or free day. Is there time you might reorganize into your "hidden" concentrated time? Look back at the time logs that you first constructed. (If that information is now much too outdated, do a new time log for yesterday, or for today.) Identify your hidden time, and decide how you will use it.

Hidden time may be moments or minutes you turn into productive use just as much as blocks of time you structure into your day. For example, you might use the five minutes you usually spent waiting for the bus, or the half hour waiting in someone's office, to plan, dictate, or read.

What you are trying to achieve is an organized life that fits in as many activities and relationships as you need, and want, without denying you the fulfillment of your own dreams. This, of course, includes time to "do nothing," e.g., thinking, daydreaming, staring into space. Basically you want to accomplish as much as the Type A (stressed) personality seems to achieve but with a Type B (relaxed) approach. A mother with three toddlers, a husband, and a full-time job will probably have to be more organized—and work harder to find hidden time—than a retired couple who seem to have nothing but time on their hands. Time is relative, however, and a 76-year-old grandmother without a job or a spouse may be more rushed, and disorganized, than her 33-year-old granddaughter with multiple obligations.

THIRTY TIME-SAVING TIPS

You now know some basic guidelines for creative and effective time management. Here, in summary form, are ways to make time work for you:

1. Prioritize. Decide on your long-term goals and set short-term priorities within those goals.
2. Concentrate. Eliminate self-made interruptions and distractions. Minimize interruptions imposed on you by others, especially phone calls and drop-in visitors.
3. Categorize your work, school, household, and personal responsibilities; focus on doing what you have to, and want to do, one day at a time.
4. Break down major tasks into small ones so: a) the work is more manageable; b) you can reward yourself as you complete each small step; c) you can keep better track of your progress; and d) you can avoid trying to do too much or at the last minute. *Set realistic deadlines for completing key projects.*
5. List all upcoming commitments or important reminders on one central calendar to facilitate planning.
6. Learn to say "no" easily and graciously.
7. Never do more than one major thing at any one moment, although you might shift back and forth among projects.
8. Develop a system for tracking your daily activities, such as a "things to do" list.
9. Periodically revise your short- and long-term goals.

10. Don't worry about the future or feel guilty about the past. Be aware of how the past teaches you, and how your current plans and efforts can improve the future.
11. If you don't know, ask someone who does.
12. Organize your home and/or office so everything is accessible, using "active" and "inactive" criteria for placement of materials.
13. Although daily expense records should be maintained, allocate a certain day each month for financial management (when bills are paid, accounts checked).
14. If you procrastinate, make sure the deadline isn't too close, and don't feel guilty about it.
15. Organize your wardrobe so you make full use of those clothes you already own.
16. Frequent stores, restaurants, service centers, or banks during non-rush or off-hour times. (You generally won't find lines at the post office when it's raining.)
17. Try to shop as infrequently as you can, avoiding last-minute dashes for a missing item.
18. Stock household goods and toiletries—nonperishable items—so shopping trips are minimized.
19. Figure out the best way to handle each situation—by phone, by mail, or in person.
20. Utilize time-saving delivery services whenever possible, including shopping over the phone and by mail.
21. Use a credit card as a time-saving convenience—not to get into debt—for over-the-phone or mail order purchases that you might otherwise have to make in person.
22. If you have a problem with lateness, time exactly how long each task (dressing, commuting, etc.) takes you, and make an appointment with yourself to leave at a certain time so you will be on time.
23. If there are major changes coming up in your life, adjust your time budget to accommodate them.
24. Promise less, deliver more.
25. Eliminate clutter. Allot time for periodic sifting and sorting: discard, give away, or sell surplus possessions.
26. As one psychologist put it: "Become more effective by becoming more inefficient." Translation: if you call people at nine a.m., because that's when *you* start working, and they're not in till ten, that's ineffective. If you get to a meeting on time and it *always* starts fifteen minutes late, that's a waste of your fifteen minutes.
27. If possible, and if appropriate, return calls and correspondence the same day.
28. Do what you have to do first, not what is easiest or most pleasant.
29. If you say to yourself, "I'll start living as soon as I finish this," you have a problem with time. Start living now, not after "this."
30. Remember that you are the master of your life—and your time.

TERMS

OK4R system   time lag

REFERENCES

ADLER, MORTIMER J., and CHARLES VAN DOREN. *How to Read a Book.* New York: Simon & Schuster, 1940, 1972. The classic work on reading effectively.

BARKAS, J.L. *How to Write Like a Professional.* New York: Arco, 1984.

FANNING, TONY, and ROBBIE FANNING. *Get It All Done and Still Be Human.* New York: Ballantine Books, 1980. How to eliminate the "time-gobblers" (telephone, television, car trips, trivia, shopping, clutter, drop-in visits, meetings, waiting, and mental blocks).

KESSELMAN-TURKEL, JUDI, and FRANKLYNN PETERSON. *Study Smarts: How to Learn More in Less Time.* Chicago, Ill.: Contemporary Books, Inc., 1981.

MCCAY, JAMES T. *The Management of Time.* Englewood Cliffs, N.J.: Prentice-Hall, Inc., 1959.

MACKENZIE, R. ALEC. *The Time Trap.* New York: McGraw-Hill Book Company, 1972.

PETERS, THOMAS J., and WATERMAN, ROBERT H., JR. *In Search of Excellence.* New York: Harper & Row, Publishers, 1982. Based on field interviews and secondary research, eight attributes are described that distinguish 75 successful and well-run American companies.

TEC, LEON. *Targets: How to Set Goals for Yourself and Reach Them.* New York: New American Library, 1980. A self-help book on setting priorities and improving time management, by the author of *The Fear of Success.*

TODD, ALDEN. *Finding Facts Fast: How to Find Out What You Want to Know Immediately.* New York: William Morrow & Company, Inc., 1972. A quick look at basic print information techniques and sources.

YOUNG, PAM and PEGGY JONES. *Catch-up on the Kitchen.* New York: Warner Books, 1983.

————. *Sidetracked Home Executives.* New York: Warner Books, 1981.

EXERCISES

1. Read any one of the books or articles cited in this book, following the OK4R system as described in this chapter.

2. Do you have a specific area in your home where you can plan, read, or study without interruptions? If you do, evaluate your "spot" as to its comfort, location, and suitability for your purpose. If not, try to create a home study.

3. Think through how you would structure your time if your situation dramatically changed—i.e. graduation, retirement, coming into a large inheritance.

(For additional exercises, checklists, and self-evaluations, see the Appendices.)

Appendices

The charts, checklists and other materials in this section are intended to help you create, and implement, a time management system to increase your effectiveness at work, school, and in your personal activities. (If you intend to make copies of any charts, first duplicate the blanks before filling out the originals.)

APPENDIX I

The ABC Approach

(A)   What You Have (Present Situation)
(B)   What You Want (Desired Outcome)
(C)   Getting What You Want by Using (A) and (B) and Asking What, When Where, Who, How, and Why (Your Plan)

(A) What You Have (Present Situation)
List your assets, liabilities, working habits, and what you enjoy doing in your leisure hours. Put yourself under a microscope—go ahead, no one else is looking—and study everything about you, from your height, weight, hair color, and clothes, to the way you crack your knuckles. Ask, and answer, questions such as:

Do I work well under pressure?
Do I project a confident image to others?
Am I confident?
Do I need deadlines to get things done?
Is my appearance pleasing?
Do I have a sense of humor?
What are my job-related skills?
What's the biggest mistake I've ever made?
What's the smartest thing I've ever done?
If I suddenly needed some money, who could I go to?
Who would I tell if I found out I had cancer?
Do I need a lot of people contact during the day?
When do I feel bored?

(B) What You Want (Desired Outcome)
List the specific goal you want to achieve, e.g., losing twenty pounds and keeping them off; writing a term paper; learning everything you can about caring for a newborn between now and eight months from now; earning $60,000 next year; being relaxed; quitting smoking once and for all; sending your youngest child to an Ivy league school, etc.

(C) Using (A) and (B) to Get What You Want (or the Who, What, Where, When, How, and Why Plan)
Take that goal and break it down into necessary interim goals. To each step, apply the What, Why, When, Where, and How questions, in that order, and devise a clear plan—with self-imposed deadlines—that will guide you in completing that plan (and achieving your goal). Remember to use (A) (e.g. financial resources, previous knowledge, access to helpful equipment or experts, etc.) as you devise your plan (C) to achieve (B).

APPENDIX II

Daily Activity Schedule

Date _____

TIME	APPOINTMENTS AND ACTIVITIES

Morning

_____   _____

_____   _____

_____   _____

Afternoon

_____   _____

_____   _____

_____   _____

Evening

_____   _____

_____   _____

_____   _____

Notes About Today:

_____

_____

_____

_____

_____

_____

_____

APPENDIX III

An Ideal Day

Use the space below to construct your ideal work or leisure day. I'll assume the beginning point and ending point; after that you're on your own.

Day of the Week _____

Wake up _____

_____

_____

_____

_____

_____

_____

_____

_____

Go to sleep _____

APPENDIX IV

Time Management Self-Evaluation

How would you rate the way you now manage your time?
(Omit any answers that are not applicable.)

Date _____

	EXCELLENT	GOOD	AVERAGE	FAIR	POOR
Work	_____	_____	_____	_____	
Personal	_____	_____	_____	_____	_____

What are the key hindrances to your effective time management?
(Check off those that apply to you.)

	WORK	SCHOOL	PERSONAL
Procrastination	_____	_____	_____
Doing too much at once	_____	_____	_____
Not prioritizing	_____	_____	_____
Inability to say "no"	_____	_____	_____
Fear of failure	_____	_____	_____
Fear of success	_____	_____	_____
Perfectionism	_____	_____	_____
Disorganization	_____	_____	_____
Complaining	_____	_____	_____
Poor planning	_____	_____	_____
Poor concentration	_____	_____	_____
Poor memory	_____	_____	_____
Watching TV	_____	_____	_____
Phone calls	_____	_____	_____
Communication skills	_____	_____	_____
Drop-in visitors	_____	_____	_____
Meetings	_____	_____	_____
Lateness	_____	_____	_____
Traveling	_____	_____	_____

Delegating   _____   _____   _____

Filing system   _____   _____   _____

Correspondence   _____   _____   _____

Sleeping habits   _____   _____   _____

Getting along with others   _____   _____   _____

Household chores   _____   _____   _____

Study skills   _____   _____   _____

Close relationships   _____   _____   _____

Others:

_____   _____   _____   _____

_____   _____   _____   _____

Pick one time waster that you checked off that you want to correct. List that choice here:

_____

Now devise a plan for correcting it:

_____

_____

_____

Target date for elimination: _____

APPENDIX V

Planning Chart

Use a chart like the one below to plan your socializing/entertainment schedule for the year, filling in any previous commitments you already know about (weddings, final exams, annual meetings). You might also use this chart, or a comparable one, for recording birthdays, anniversaries, and similar dates that you have to remember each year.

Planning Calendar

January	February	March
April	May	June
July	August	September
October	November	December

APPENDIX VI

Student Checklist

How many of the following questions can you answer "yes" to?

	Yes	Sometimes	No
1. I have a regular schedule for studying.	_____	_____	_____
2. I have a specific place I always use to study.	_____	_____	_____
3. I always get the course requirements before the semester begins so I can buy books ahead and plan.	_____	_____	_____
4. My social life is planned around my exam schedule and required papers.	_____	_____	_____
5. I start papers—planning/researching—as soon as they are assigned.	_____	_____	_____
6. I always have time to do extra readings in the areas I'm interested in.	_____	_____	_____
7. I enjoy school—except for tests and papers.	_____	_____	_____

Devise a plan to turn every *no* or *sometimes* into a *yes.*

APPENDIX VII

Time Management for Teachers

Based on the organizing principle of doing repetitive tasks once, political science professor Ernest Evans, at Catholic University in Washington, D.C., has these suggestions for professors:

1. Since students generally have certain standard questions about careers or requirements for their major field, I suggest developing a four- to six-page typed memo in answer to each of these questions. Have a stack of memos available to give out in response to students' standard questions. Tell them to come back after they have read it if they want to discuss any further questions.

2. Develop and have on hand copies of short reading lists for those topics that students are most likely to ask about.

3. Type up your lecture notes so you can photocopy them for students who have missed a lecture. This copy can supplement a friend's notes that they should consult as well. [JLB note: It is important to avoid the abuse of this time-saving system as a stimulus for students to skip classes.]

4. If you are an expert on certain topics, and reporters call on you for quotes, write up summaries of your views on a few frequently asked questions. Unless a reporter has a deadline problem, you can mail out your written comments, saving you time and lessening the likelihood of misquotes.

APPENDIX VIII

Creating Your Own Time Management Solutions

Apply what you have learned about time management in this book to tasks in your work or personal life that you could handle more creatively and efficiently. Use the space below to write down at least two time-saving techniques that you will use to improve your life:

1. _____

   _____

   _____

   _____

   _____

   _____

2. _____

   _____

   _____

   _____

   _____

   _____

Index

ABC approach, 4, 11, 17, 127, 138
Active, v, 58–9, 93–4, 135
Activity sheet, 84
Adler, Alfred, 43, 44
Aerobics, 14. *See also* Exercise
AE people, 5
Agenda, 79
Aikman, Ann, 14, 18
American Adventurers Association, 108
American Youth Hostels, 108
Asimov, Isaac, 23
Aslett, Don, 97–8, 101
Assignments
  getting, 24, 126
  keeping track of, 127
Association of Family Conciliation Courts, 36
Association of Part-Time Professionals, 133

Barbach, Lonnie, 38
Bicycle Manufacturers Association of
    America, Inc., 41
Billson, Janet Mancini, 116
Bliss, Edwin C., 84, 86
Body mirroring, 115
Bookcases, 61–3
Books, 61–3
Breaks
  efficiency, 76–7
  goofing off, 77. *See* Procrastination
Brunch, 110
Burnout, 6, 17
Busywork, 53–4

Calendar, planning, 57, 127, 135, 143

Calisthenics. *See* Exercise
Career. *See* Work
Catalyst, 133
Change, 42–4, 135, 136
Child. *See* Children
Children, 3, 6, 94–5, 112–7, 130–33
The Cinderella Complex, Colette Dowling,
    36–7, 44
Cleaning, 91–2, 97–9, 107, 110
Clock, 4–5, 6, 77
Closets, 93–4
Clutter, 94, 135
Cohen, Stanley N., 35–6
Communication
  at home, 114–7, 119
  at work, 81–3
  facilitative, 115, 118
  nonverbal, 82, 114–5
  obstructive, 115, 118
Commuting, 10, 21, 39–42, 123
Complaining, 21, 28–9
Compulsive talkers, 29, 79–80
Computer, 73, 124–5
Concentration, 134
Conferences, 79
Confidence, 29, 37, 140
Cooker
  slow, 100, 101
  rice, 100
Cooper, Kenneth H., 14
Correspondence, 9, 58, 71–3, 87, 135
Criticism, inability to take, 21, 37–9
  solutions, 38–9

Davis, Flora, 12–13, 17
Deadlines, 3, 125, 134–5, 142
Decision-making skills, 53
Decorating, 95–7
Delegating, 52, 77–8, 87, 94, 102, 125
Desk, 60–1
   inside, 60
   on top, 61
Devaluing, 21, 32
Diamond, Lynn, 24, 38
Diet, 9, 10, 13, 106, 141
Directories, household, 99
Disorganization. *See* Organization
"Do" lists. *See* Lists
Doing too much at once, 21, 22–3, 134
Double bind, 82
Douglass, Merrill E., 40–1, 55
Dowling, Colette, 36–7, 44
"Drop in" visitor. *See* Visitor interruptions
Drucker, Peter F., 30, 48
Duck, Steve, 111, 118
Dyad, 81–3, 115

Efficiency breaks, 76–7
Ellis, Albert, 25, 44–5, 80
Energy, 12–4
Entertaining, 91, 123
Errands, 98–9, 106, 135
Evans, Ernest, 145
"Everything Notebook," 58
Exercise, 13, 40–1, 84, 106–7, 119, 132
   creating plan, 10, 40–1, 106–7, 119
   reasons for, 10–11
   types of, 13, 14, 107, 119, 132

Failure, fear of, 21, 22, 25, 29–30, 33, 92
   solution to, 29–30
Family, 3, 5, 7, 42, 112–4
Fatigue, 13–14, 17
Fear of failure. *See* Failure, fear of
Fear of success. *See* Success, fear of
Feedback, 116–7, 118
File systems, 58–60
"First Inquiry." *See* Mayo, Elton
Fischer, Theodore, 58
Flexible working hours. *See* Flexitime
Flexitime, 70–1
Floor coverings, 97
Food
   canned, 101
   clean-up, 101
   frozen, 100–101
   preparation, 99–100
   processor, 100
   stocking, 101
   See also Diet, overeating
Franklin, Benjamin, 2

Free-lance. *See* Self-employed
Freyberg, Joan, 35
Friends, 3, 5, 6, 22, 36, 42, 85, 105, 109, 119
Friendship, 3, 8, 110–11, 118

Gilliatt, Mary, 96, 102
Glass, John, 117
Goals
   long-term, 8, 42, 51, 52, 83, 124, 134
   setting of, 7–8, 16, 83, 87, 134, 142
   short-range, 11, 14–6, 51, 52, 53–4, 124, 134
Goldfein, Donna, 40, 132–3
Guests. *See* Entertaining

Habits
   bad, 21, 42–4
Hall, Edward T., 5, 18
Hawthorne Effect, 85
Heloise, 102
"Hidden" time, 133–4
Hobby, 107, 108–9, 120
Homemakers, 7, 13, 91–2, 117, 130–33
Home office, 63–4, 126, 133
Hopi Indians, 5
Household
   chores, 6, 84, 85, 91–102, 131–2, 135
   errands, 98–9, 135
   maintenance, 91, 97–101
   responsibilities, 91–2, 94–5
Housewife. *See* Homemaker
Housework. *See* Household, chores

Ideal day, 18, 140
Impatience, 21, 34–5
Inability to say "no," 21, 23–5, 46, 134
Inactive, 58–9, 93–4, 135
Innovative Information Techniques, 24, 38
In Search of Excellence, Peters and Waterman, Jr., 136
Interruptions
   self-made, 21–44, 134
   telephone, 73–5, 133, 134
   visitor, 75–6, 109, 134
Intimacy, 8, 110–7
Inventory. *See* Time log

Jealousy, 21, 36–7
Jones, Peggy, 43, 132, 136

Keats, John, 104
Kesselman-Turkel, Judi, 128, 136
Kipling, Rudyard, 68
Kitchen, 93–4, 99–101
Knaus, William J., 25, 44–5
Korda, Michael, 71, 86

Lakein, Alan, 8, 18, 72
Lang, Doe, 29, 45

Lateness, 11, 135
Laundry, 97, 99, 107
Leisure, 4, 6, 10, 22, 64–5, 105–20, 140
Letters. *See* Correspondence
Lindemann, Carol, 31
Lists
    check, 52, 81, 141–42, 144
    for entertaining, 110
    "to do," 23, 51, 54–6, 94
Love, 21, 35–6
Low frustration tolerance, 21, 25, 34–5
Lowell, Florence, 110, 119

Machlowitz, Marilyn M., 80–1, 86
Mackenzie, Alex, 11, 18, 45
Magazines, 39, 61–3, 87
Magnetic diskette, 58, 65
Mail. *See* Correspondence
Maltz, Maxwell, 43
Mayo, Elton, 76–7, 85
McQuade, Walter, 14, 18
Meetings, 52, 78–9, 84, 135
Menus, 101, 102
Mistakes, 30, 142
Murphy's law, 110

**National Association for Professional
    Saleswomen, 41**
Network. *See* Networking
Networking, 110–11
Newspapers. *See* Reading
Nine-to-fivers, 6, 69–87, 117, 123–5
Nonverbal communication, 114–5, 117
Notetaking, 128–9

Oakley, Ann, 91, 102, 131
Office
    home, 63–4, 126, 133
    workers, 5, 69–87, 123–7, 131–3
Offit, Avodah, 112, 119
OK4R System, 128, 135, 136
One Minute Manager, Blanchard and Johnson,
    38, 44
Organized. *See* Organization
Organization, 44, 48–66, 134–5
    at home, 93–4
    at work, 50–63
    disorganization, 44, 50, 64
    getting organized, 134–5
    of wardrobe, 135
    principles of, 54–7, 58–9
Overeating, 3. *See also* Diet
Overvaluing, 21, 32

Paint
    oil-based alkyd, 96, 101
    water-based latex, 96, 101
Painting, 96–7

Paperwork, 71–3
Paradox, 82, 85
Parenting. *See* Children
Parenting seminars, 131
Pareto. *See* Pareto's 80/20 Principle
Pareto's 80/20 Principle, 17–8, 124
Partner, 42, 112–7
Party, 3, 4, 57, 110, 119
Pauk, Walter, 128
Perfectionism, 21, 22, 32–4, 81, 92, 112
    solution to, 33–4
Peterson, Franklynn, 128, 136
Phobia. *See* Fear of success, Fear of failure
Phone. *See* Telephone
Photography, 108–9, 129
Planning, 11–2, 13, 39, 51–2, 100, 102, 124,
    134
    reasons for, 3–6, 124
    without interruption, 136
    See also Calendar
Pletcher, Barbara, 41
Plutarch, 137
Postprandial dip, 13, 17
Principle
    organizing, 50, 54–6, 57, 65
    Pareto's 80/20, 17, 124
    verb-noun, 15–7
Priorities, 3, 15, 16, 23
    long-term, 51, 52
    short-term, 11, 14–6, 51, 52, 53–4
Procrastination, 20, 22, 25–8, 71, 129–30, 135
    solution to, 25–7
Professor. *See* Teacher
Progress reports, 83–5
Promises, 64, 135
Promptness, 51. *See also* Lateness
PROPLAN, 124–5
Psychotherapy, 36, 43

"Quiet hour," 75

Reactive, v
Reading
    assignment, 136
    finding time for, 42, 65
    newspapers, 9, 39, 61, 132–3
    organization of materials, 61–3
    without interruption, 136
Recreation, 106–111
Relationships, 8, 37, 109–117
    love, 8. *See also* Children, Intimacy, Spouse
Relaxation, 84, 106–9, 130
    See also Stress, Fatigue, Workaholism,
        Burnout
Relaxed, 4, 42, 134, 142
Repairs, 96–7
Reports, 79, 83–5

Richardson, Gisele, 113, 119
Ronen, Simcha, 70
Rutherford, Robert D., 11, 18

Scheduling, 11–12, 52
Schiffman, Muriel, 79–80
Scott, Dru, 23, 45
Sedlacek, Keith, 14, 18, 40
Self-employed, 56, 117, 125–7
Self-evaluations, 52, 81, 141–42, 144
Self-fulfilling prophesy, 82
Sex, 3, 10, 112
Sheenan, James T., 106, 119
Shopping, 91, 99–101, 135
Sidetracked Home Executives, Young and Jones,
   43, 132, 136
Sierra Club, 108
"SIP," 116, 118
Sleep, 10, 12–3, 39, 41
Slow cooker, 100
Socializing, 41, 78, 109–114
   how to, 109–10
   making time for, 109, 130
Speedreading, 128
Speedwriting, 128
Sports. *See* Exercise
Spouse. *See* Partner
Steffen, R. James, 23, 45
Stocking supplies, 60, 101
Strayhorn, Joseph M., Jr., 115, 119
Stress, 13–14, 17–8, 40, 134
Structure
   need for, 123
   of time, 123–34
Student, 13, 117, 127–30, 144
   older, 129
Studying, 6, 123, 128–30, 136
Success
   fear of, 21, 22, 25, 30, 31–2, 33, 92
   solution to, 31–2
Superiors, dealing with, 10, 78
Support systems, 36, 110–11

Tape recorder, 40
Teacher, 13–4, 146
Tec, Leon, 31, 45
Telephone, 21, 42, 51, 54, 71, 73–5, 87,
   133, 135
Television, 21, 25, 42, 107–8, 109, 132
Tennov, Dorothy, 115, 119
Test anxiety, 129–30
Theophratus, 122
"Things to do" lists. *See* Lists, "to do"
Tickler file, 59–60
Time
   alone, 113–4, 118
   budget, 5
   concept of, 4–5

creative, 3, 6–7, 39, 117, 146
   diffused, 113, 118
   hidden, 133–4
   personal, 105–20
   qualitative, 113, 118
   structuring, 123–33
Time lag, 126, 135
Time log, 9, 17, 18, 98
Time management
   as skill, 4
   at work, 123–7, 134–5
   creative, 3, 117
   household, 97–8
   identifying strengths, 51–3
   inventories, 8–11, 17, 18, 98
   personal, 105–20
   setting goals to facilitate, 87, 124
   tips, 134–5
Time Management Center, 40, 55
Time off, 5, 76
   See also Leisure
Time wasters, 15, 21–47
   bad habits, 21, 42–4
   being in love, other emotional afflictions,
      21, 35–6
   commuting and travel, 10, 21, 39–42,
      108–9, 123
   complaining, 21, 28–9
   devaluing (or overvaluing) activities, 21,
      32
   doing too much at once, 21, 22–3
   fear of failure, 21, 22, 25, 29–30, 33
   fear of success, 21, 22, 25, 30, 31–2, 33
   inability to say "no," 21, 23–5, 46, 134
   inability to take criticism, 21, 37–9
   jealousy, 21, 36–7
   perfectionism, 21, 22, 32–4
   procrastination, 20, 22, 25–8, 71, 129–30,
      135
   telephone, 21, 42, 51, 54, 71, 73–5, 133, 135
   television, 21, 25, 42
Transportation. *See* Travel
Travel, 8, 10, 38–42, 108–9, 123
Triad, 81–3, 115–6
TV. *See* Television
Type A personality, 14, 134
Type B personality, 134
Typewriter, 73

Vacation, 3, 5, 51, 85, 87, 108, 112, 117 125
VCR. *See* Video recorder
Verb-noun principle, 15–16, 56
Video recorder, 35, 108–9

Waiting. *See* **Lateness**
Waldo, Kay Cronkite, 11, 18, 45
Wall coverings, 96–7
Weiner, Ron, 124–5

Wheelis, Alan, 42, 45
Wilkinson, William C., 41
Wilmot, William W., 82, 86
Winston, Stephanie, 63, 65
Word processor, 73, 86
Work, 68–87
   getting to, 8–10, 39–41
   part-time, 133

   time at, 69–87
Workaholism, 6, 17, 80–81

Young, Edward, 21
Young, Pam, 43, 132, 136

Zerof, Herbert G., 112, 119
Zerubavel, Eviatar, 5, 18